D0211658

Improve Your Memory

3rd Edition

By
Ron Fry

CAREER PRESS
3 Tice Road
P.O. Box 687
Franklin Lakes, NJ 07417
1-800-CAREER-1
201-848-0310 (NJ and outside U.S.)
FAX: 201-848-1727

IMPROVE YOUR MEMORY, 3RD EDITION

ISBN 1-56414-231-0, $6.99

Cover design by The Visual Group

Printed in the U.S.A. by Book-mart Press

To order this title by mail, please include price as noted above, $2.50 handling per order, and $1.00 for each book ordered. Send to: Career Press, Inc., 3 Tice Road, P.O. Box 687, Franklin Lakes, NJ 07417.

Or call toll-free 1-800-CAREER-1 (NJ and Canada: 201-848-0310) to order using VISA or MasterCard, or for further information on books from Career Press.

Library of Congress Cataloging-in-Publication Data

Fry, Ronald W.
    Improve your memory / by Ron Fry. -- 3rd ed.
        p.   cm. -- (Ron Fry's how to study program)
    Includes index.
    ISBN 1-56414-231-0 (paper)
    1. Mnemonics. 2. Memory. I. Title. II. Series: Fry, Ronald W.
How to study program.
BF385.F79 1996
153.1'4--dc20   96-15758
                                                          CIP

Contents

Foreword

Something to remember

This year marks another major milestone in the near-decade long evolution of my *How to Study Program*—the addition of two new titles (*Get Organized* and *Use Your Computer*) as well as the reissuance of new editions of *How to Study* (its fourth), *Improve Your Writing*, *Improve Your Reading*, *Improve Your Memory* and *"Ace" Any Test* (all in third editions). *Take Notes* and *Manage Your Time*, both still available in second editions, were not updated this year.

Why are these books the best-selling series of study guides ever published? Why are they still so *needed*, not only by students but by the parents who want so badly for them to do well?

Because virtually all of the conditions I've been writing and speaking about across the country since 1988 have remained...or gotten *worse:*

1. Despite modest recent improvements in test scores—in 1995, the average on the verbal portion of the SAT rose five points and the math scores improved an average of three points— U.S. students still score abysmally low compared to many other countries, especially on science and math tests.

2. Most parents, when polled, say improving our public schools is our nation's number one priority. Those same parents do *not* think public schools are doing a very good job teaching their kids much of anything.

3. Business leaders continue to complain that far too many entry-level job candidates can barely read, write, add or multiply. Many can't fill out job applications! As a result, businesses are spending billions to teach employees the basic skills everyone agrees they should have learned in school.

It's almost inevitable that these conditions will *continue to worsen*. In just the next four years (i.e., by the year 2000), 7 million kids will enter school, increasing the number of students in U.S. elementary and high schools to more than 50 million. This is an increase that rivals the one caused by the boomer generation.

Unfortunately for this new crop of students, the money to fund their education just isn't there. Given the current state of the federal budget and most states' situations, these students probably face budget *cuts* all around. Voters aren't exactly lining up at the polls to fund new schools and pay teachers higher salaries.

This means that the old problems that most affect students' ability to learn—overcrowded classrooms, lack of resources (especially computers and other new technologies), lack of qualified teachers—will continue to frustrate students who want to learn but need help.

As a result, the need for my nine books will, unfortunately, continue, since they offer *exactly* the help most students need and their parents demand.

So who are you?

A number of you are students, not just the high school students I always thought were my readers, but also college students (a rousing plug for their high school preparation) and *junior* high school students (which says something far more positive about their motivation and eventual success).

Many of you are adults returning to school, and some of you are long out of school, but if you could learn *now* the study skills your teachers never taught you, you would do better in your careers—especially if you knew how recall the key points you'll need to make in your presentation or remember the new clients' names.

All too many of you are parents with the same lament: "How do I get Jill to do better in school? She can't remember my birthday, let alone when her next trig test is."

I want to briefly take the time to address every one of the audiences for this book and discuss some of the factors particular to each of you:

If you're a high school student

You should be particularly comfortable with both the language and format of this book—its relatively short sentences and paragraphs, occasionally humorous (hopefully) headings and subheadings, a reasonable but certainly not outrageous vocabulary. I wrote it with you in mind!

If you're a junior high school student

It doesn't do much good to figure out how to study if you can't remember anything that you've just read, so learning to improve your memory is definitely key. You are trying to learn how to study at *precisely* the right time. Sixth, seventh and eighth grades—before that sometimes cosmic leap to high school—are without a doubt the period in which all these study skills should be mastered. If you're serious enough about studying to be reading this book, I doubt you'll have trouble with the concepts or the language.

If you're a "traditional" college student...

...somewhere in the 18 to 25 age range, I would have hoped you had already learned all of the study techniques, especially basic memory techniques. If not (and even if you know some tips but not every trick and gimmick covered in this book), I guarantee that truly mastering these memory techniques will help you long after you graduate (with As, of course!).

If you're the parent of a student of any age

Your child's school is probably doing little if anything to teach him or her how to study. Which means he or she is not learning how to *learn*. And that means he or she is not learning how to *succeed*.

Should the schools be accomplishing that? Absolutely. After all, we spend $275 billion on elementary and secondary education in this country, *an average of $6,000 per* *student per year*. We ought to be getting more for that money than possible graduation, some football cheers and a rotten entry-level job market.

What can parents do?

There are probably even more dedicated parents out there than dedicated students, since the first phone call at any of my radio or TV appearances comes from a sincere and worried parent asking, "What can I do to help my kid do better in school?" Okay, here they are, the rules for parents of students of any age:

1. **Set up a homework area.** Free of distraction, well lit, all necessary supplies handy.

2. **Set up a homework routine.** When and where it gets done. Same bat-time every day.

3. **Set homework priorities**. Actually, just make the point that homework *is* the priority—before a date, before TV, before going out to play, whatever.

4. **Make reading a habit**—for them, certainly, but also for yourselves, presuming it isn't already. Kids will inevitably do what you *do*, not what you *say* (even if you say *not* to do what you *do*). So if you keep nagging them to read while *you* turn on the eighth sitcom of the night, what message do you think you're giving them?

5. **Turn off the TV.** Or, at the very least, severely limit when and how much TV-watching is appropriate. This may be the toughest one. Believe me, I'm the father of a 7-year old. I know. Do your best.

6. **Talk to the teachers.** Find out what your kids are supposed to be learning. If you don't, you can't really supervise. You might even be teaching them things at odds with what the teacher's trying to do.

7. **Encourage and motivate**, but don't nag them to do their homework. It doesn't work.

8. **Supervise their work**, but don't fall into the trap of *doing* their homework.

9. **Praise them to succeed**, but don't overpraise them for mediocre work. Kids know when you're slinging it. Be wary of any school or teacher that is more worried about your kid's "self esteem" than her grades, skills and abilities. I'm not advocating the withdrawal of kudos for good work, but kids need to get the message that "you get what you pay for"; that you need to work hard to actually *earn* rewards. Horror stories about teachers giving out good grades, reducing standards or not assigning homework because they're afraid some of the kids will "feel bad" if they don't do well are exactly that—horrible, scary stories. Such tactics merely set kids up for *bigger* failures down the road in a world that puts a premium on your skills and abilities and doesn't seem to care very much how you "feel" about it.

10. **Convince them of reality.** (This is for older students.) Okay, I'll admit it's almost as much of a stretch as turning off the TV, but learning and believing that the real world will not care about their grades but measure them solely by what they know and what they can do is a lesson that

will save many tears (probably yours). It's probably never too early to (carefully) let your boy or girl genius get the message that life is not fair. Which is why teaching them resilience and determination—so they'll pick themselves up, dust themselves off and try again when they fail—is paramount.

11. **If you can afford it, get your kid(s) a computer** and all the software they can handle. Many people have been saying it for years (including me) and there really is no avoiding it: Your kids, whatever their age, absolutely must master technology (computers) in order to survive, let alone succeed, in school and after school. There's even new empirical data to back up all the braying: a recent decade-long study has shown that kids who master computers learn faster and earn higher test scores.

The importance of your involvement

Don't for a minute underestimate the importance of *your* commitment to your child's success: Your involvement in your child's education is absolutely essential to his or her eventual success.

Surprisingly enough, the results of every study done in the last two decades about what affects a child's success in school clearly demonstrate that only one factor *overwhelmingly* affects it, every time: parental involvement. Not the size of the school, the money spent per pupil, the number of language labs, how many of the students go on to college, how many great teachers there are (or lousy ones). All factors, yes. *But none as significant as the effect you can have*.

So please, take the time to read this book (and all of the others in the series, but especially *How to Study*) yourself. Learn what your kids *should* be learning (and which of the other subject-specific books in the series your child needs the most).

And you can help tremendously, *even if you were not a great student yourself, even if you never learned great study skills*. You can learn now with your child—not only will it help him or her in school, it will help *you* on the job, whatever your field.

If you're a nontraditional student

If you're going back to high school, college or graduate school at age 25, 45, 65 or 85—you probably need the help these nine books offer more than anyone! Why? Because the longer you've been out of school, the more likely you don't remember what you've forgotten. And you've probably forgotten what you're supposed to remember! As much as I emphasize that it's rarely too early to learn good study habits, I must also emphasize that it's never too *late*.

If you're returning to school and attempting to carry even a partial load of courses while simultaneously holding down a job, raising a family, or both, there are some particular problems you face that you probably didn't the first time you were in school:

Time and money pressures. Let's face it, when all you had to worry about was going to school, it simply *had* to be easier than going to school, raising a family and working for a living simultaneously. (And it was!) Mastering all of the techniques of time management is even more essential if you are to effectively juggle your many responsibilities to your career, family, clubs, friends, etc., with your commitment to school. Money management may well be another essential skill, whether figuring out how to pay for child care (something you probably didn't have to worry about the last time you were in school) or how to manage all your responsibilities while cutting your hours at work to make time for school.

Self-imposed fears of inadequacy. You may well convince yourself that you're just "out of practice" with all this school stuff. You don't even remember what to do with a highlighter! While some of this fear is valid, most is not. The valid part is that you are returning to an academic atmosphere, one that you may not have even visited for a decade or two. And it *is* different (which I'll discuss more below) than the "work-a-day" world. That's just a matter of adjustment and, trust me, it will take a matter of days, if not hours, to dissipate. But I suspect what many of you are really fearing is that you just aren't in that school "mentality" anymore, that you don't "think" the same way. Or, perhaps more pertinently to this book, that the skills you need to succeed in school are rusty.

I think these last fears are groundless. You've been out there thinking and doing for quite a few years, perhaps very successfully, so it's really ridiculous to think school will be so different. It won't be. Relax. And while you may think your study skills are rusty, as we discussed earlier, you've probably been using them every day in your career. Even if I can't convince you, you have my **How to Study Program**, your refresher course. It will probably teach you more about studying than you ever forgot.

Maybe you're worried because you didn't exactly light up the academic power plant the first time around. Well, neither did Edison or Einstein or a host of other relatively successful people. But then, you've changed rather significantly since those halcyon days of "boola boolaing," haven't you? Held a series of jobs, raised a family, saved money, taken on more and more responsibility? Concentrate on how much *more* qualified you are for school *now* than you were *then!*

Feeling you're "out of your element." This is a slightly different fear, the fear that you just don't fit in any more. After all, you're not 18 again. But then, neither are fully half the college students on campus today. That's right, fully 50 percent of all college students are older than 25. The reality is, you'll probably feel more in your element now than you did the first time around!

You'll see teachers differently. Probably a plus. It's doubtful you'll have the same awe you did the first time around. At worst, you'll consider teachers your equals. At best, you'll consider them younger and not necessarily as successful or experienced as you are. In either event, you probably won't be quite as ready to treat your college professors as if they were close relatives of the Almighty.

There *are* differences in academic life. It's slower than the "real" world, and you may well be moving significantly faster than its normal pace. When you were 18, an afternoon without classes meant a game of Frisbee. Now it might mean catching up on a week's worth of errands, cooking (and freezing) a week's worth of dinners and/or writing four reports due last week. Despite your own hectic schedule, do not expect campus life to accelerate in response. You will have to get used to people and systems with far less interest in speed.

Some random thoughts about learning

Learning shouldn't be painful and certainly doesn't have to be boring, though it's far too often both. However, it's not necessarily going to be wonderful and painless, either. Sometimes you actually have to work hard to figure something out or get a project done. That *is* reality.

It's also reality that everything isn't readily apparent or easily understandable. Confusion reigns. Tell yourself that's okay and learn how to get past it. Heck, if you actually think you understand everything you've read the first time through, you're kidding yourself. Learning something slowly doesn't mean there's something wrong with you. It may be a subject that virtually everybody learns slowly. A good student doesn't panic when something doesn't seem to be getting through the haze. He just takes his time, follows whatever steps apply and remains confident that the light bulb will indeed inevitably go on.

Parents often ask me, "How can I motivate my teenager?" My initial response is usually to say, "If I knew the answer to that question, I would have retired very wealthy quite some time ago." However, I think there *is* an answer, but it's not something *parents* can do, it's something you, the student, have to decide: Are you going to spend the school day interested and alert or bored and resentful?

It's really that simple. Why not develop the attitude that you have to go to school anyway, so rather than being bored or miserable while you're there, you might as well be active and learn as much as possible? The difference between a C and an A or B for many students is, I firmly believe, merely a matter of wanting to do better. As I constantly stress in interviews, inevitably you will leave school. And very quickly, you'll discover the premium is on what you know and what you can do. Grades won't count anymore, neither will tests. So you can learn it all now or regret it later.

How many times have you said to yourself, "I don't know why I'm bothering trying to learn this (calculus, algebra, geometry, physics, chemistry, history, whatever). I'll *never* use this again!"? I hate to burst bubbles, but unless you've got a patent on some great new fortune-telling device, you have *no clue* what you're going to need to know tomorrow or next week, let alone next year or next decade.

I've been amazed in my own life how things I did with no specific purpose in mind (except probably to earn money) turned out years later to be not just invaluable to my life or career but essential. How was I to know when I took German as my language elective in high school that the most important international trade show in book publishing, my field, was in Frankfurt...Germany? Or that the basic skills I learned one year working for an accountant (while I was writing my first book) would become essential when I later started four companies? Or how important basic math skills would be in selling and negotiating over the years? (Okay, I'll admit it: I haven't used a differential equation in 20 years, but, hey, you never know!)

So learn it *all*. And don't be surprised if the subject you'd vote "least likely to ever be useful" winds up being the key to *your* fame and fortune.

There are other study guides

Though I immodestly maintain my *How to Study Program* to be the most helpful to the most people, there are certainly lots of other purported study books out there. Unfortunately, I don't think many of them deliver what they promise. In fact, I'm actually getting mad at the growing number of study guides out there claiming to be "the sure way to straight As" or something of the sort. These are also the books that dismiss reasonable alternative ways to study and learn with, "Well, that never worked for me," as if that is a valid reason to dismiss it, as if we should *care* that it didn't work for the author.

Inevitably, these books promote the authors' "system," which usually means what *they* did to get through school.

This "system," whether basic and traditional or wildly quirky, may or may not work for you. So what do you do if "their" way of taking notes makes no sense to you? Or you master their highfalutin "Super Student Study Symbols" and still get Cs?

I'm not getting into a Dennis Miller rant here, but there are very few "rights" and "wrongs" out there in the study world. There's certainly no single "right" way to attack a multiple choice test or absolute "right" way to take notes. So don't get fooled into thinking there *is*, especially if what you're doing seems to be working for you. Don't change what ain't broke because some self-proclaimed study guru claims what you're doing is all wet. Maybe he's all wet. After all, if his system works for you, all it *really* means is you have the same likes, dislikes, talents or skills as the author.

Needless to say, don't read *my* books looking for the Truth—that single, inestimable system of "rules" that works for everyone. You won't find it, 'cause there's no such bird. You *will* find a plethora of techniques, tips, tricks, gimmicks and what-have-you, some or all of which may work for you, some of which won't. Pick and choose, change and adapt, figure out what works for you. Because *you* are the one responsible for creating *your* study system, *not me*.

Yes, I'll occasionally point out "my way" of doing something. I may even suggest that I think it offers some clear advantages to all the alternative ways of accomplishing the same thing. But that *doesn't* mean it's some carved-in-stone, deviate-from-the-sacred-Ron-Fry-study-path-under-penalty-of-a-writhing-death kind of rule.

I've used the phrase "Study smarter, not harder" as a sort of catch-phrase in promotion and publicity for the **How to Study Program** for nearly a decade. So what does it mean to you? Does it mean I guarantee you'll spend less time studying? Or that the least amount of time is best? Or that studying isn't ever supposed to be hard?

Hardly. It means that studying inefficiently is wasting time that could be spent doing other (okay, probably more *fun)* things and that getting your studying done as quickly and efficiently as possible is a realistic, worthy and *attainable* goal. I'm no stranger to hard work, but I'm not a monastic dropout who thrives on self-flagellation. I try not to work harder than I have to!

What you'll remember from this one

If you have trouble remembering your own phone number, this is the book for you. This new edition is even more complete—a simple, practical, easy-to-use memory book that will help you:

- Remember numbers.
- Remember dates and facts.
- Retain more of what you read the *first* time you read it.
- Take notes that will help you score well on tests and term papers.
- Remember numbers.
- Build a bigger vocabulary.
- Remember how to spell.
- Remember names and faces.
- Remember numbers. (I get the feeling this is *everyone's* biggest problem!)

What's more, **Improve Your Memory** will help you do *all* of this without a mind-numbing amount of time and effort. Its advice is easy to learn and even easier to apply.

Along the way, you might even develop the skills for knowing at all times where you've left your glasses, car keys or wallet.

The best way to approach this book is to read Chapters 1 through 10 straight through, then go back and review some of the mechanics of memory improvement contained in Chapters 3 through 10. If you have ADD—or are the parent of someone who does—be sure to read Chapter 11.

After this review, take the test in Chapter 12 and see how much you've improved *your* memory. I'm sure you'll be amazed. When you've finished this book, you'll be effortlessly flexing mental muscles you never knew you had!

In case you were wondering

Before we get on with all the tips and techniques necessary to remember anything you need to, *when* you need to, let me make two important points about all nine study books.

First, I believe in gender equality, in writing as well as in life. Unfortunately, I find constructions such as "he and she," "s/he," "womyn" and other such stretches to be sometimes painfully awkward. I have therefore attempted to sprinkle pronouns of both genders throughout the text.

Second, you will find many pieces of advice, examples, lists and other phrases and sections spread throughout two or more of the nine books. Certainly **How to Study**, which is an overview of all the study skills, necessarily contains, though in summarized form, some of each of the other eight books.

The repetition is unavoidable. While I urge everyone to read all nine books in the series, but especially **How to Study**, they *are* nine individual books. And many people only buy one of them. Consequently, I must include in each the pertinent material *for that topic*, even if that material is then repeated in a second or even a third book.

That said, I can guarantee that the nearly 1,200 pages of my *How to Study Program* contain the most wide-ranging, comprehensive and complete system of studying ever published. I have attempted to create a system that is usable, that is useful, that is practical, that is learnable. One that *you* can use—whatever your age, whatever your level of achievement, whatever your IQ—to start doing better in school, in work and in life *immediately*.

Ron Fry
May 1996

Chapter 1

Thank you, Zbigniew

Which do you think you're more likely to remember—your first date with your future spouse (even if it was decades ago) or what you had for breakfast last Thursday?

Probably the former (though not if last Thursday was your first experiment with yak butter).

Which event conjures up the most memories—the Blizzard of 1996 or the last time it rained (unless, of course, it *really* poured cats and dogs)?

Which name would you find difficult to forget—Joe Smith or Zbigniew Brzezinski? We'll deal with how to remember *spelling* old Zbig in Chapters 5 and 7.

What do all the "memorable" names, dates, places and events have in common? The fact that they're *different*. What makes something memorable is its *extra*ordinariness, how much it differs from our normal experiences.

The reason so many of us forget where we put the car keys or our eyeglasses is that putting these objects down is the most ordinary of occurrences, part and parcel of the most humdrum aspects of our lives. We have trouble remembering facts and formulas from books and classroom lectures for the same reason. To be schooled is to be bombarded with facts day in and day out. How do you make those facts memorable? (By the way, has anyone seen my glasses?)

Beef up your RAM

In order to understand how to make the important facts memorable, how to keep them stored safely at least until final exams, let's first take a look at how the brain and, more specifically, memory work.

I'm going to call upon a rather useful, and for that reason somewhat overused analogy, and ask you to think of your brain as that computer you typed your last paper on—an organic computer, wired with nerves, hooked up to various INPUT devices (your five senses) and possessed of both ROM (read-only memory) and RAM (random access memory).

The ROM is the data you can't touch—the disk-operating system, the information that tells your heart to pump and your lungs to breathe.

On the other hand, RAM is much more accessible. Like most PCs nowadays, your brain stores RAM in two places: *short-term* memory (that old single-sided, low density floppy disk you've been meaning to get rid of) and *long-term* memory (that 1-gigabyte baby on the hard drive).

Okay, so what happens to INPUT in this system?

A matter of choice

Given the bombardment of data we receive every day, our brains constantly are making choices. Data either goes in one ear and out the other, or it stops in short-term memory. But when that old floppy disk gets full, the brain is left with a choice—jettison some old information or pass it on to the hard drive.

How does it make a decision *which* information to pass on and *where* to store it?

Well, scientists aren't positive about this yet, but, of course, they have theories.

The most readily stored and accessed is data that's been *rehearsed*—gone over again and again. Most of us readily access our knowledge of how to read, how to drive, the year Columbus "discovered" America, the name of the first president of the United States and other basics without any difficulty at all. (At worst, you remember "Columbus sailed the ocean blue in 1492.") We've worn familiar paths through our memory banks accessing this type of information or skill.

Why, then, can some people recite the names, symbols and atomic weights of the elements of the periodic table— while they're playing (and winning) Trivial Pursuit—as easily as they can the date of Columbus's dubious achievement?

To return to our computer analogy, this information has gotten "tagged" or "coded" in some way so that it can be easily retrieved by the user. For instance, before storing a file in your computer's long-term RAM, you give it a name, one that will easily conjure what exactly that file is. In other words, you make the file *stand out* in some way from the host of other files you've stored on your disk drive.

For some people, myriad bits of data are almost automatically tagged so that they can be quite easily and handily stored and retrieved. But most of us, if we are to have exceptional memories, must make a special effort.

Can you twist and shout...and remember?

First and foremost, there are three very different kinds of memory—visual, verbal and kinesthetic, *each* of which can be strong or weak and only the first two of which are associated with your *brain*.

Most people have the easiest time strengthening their *visual* memories, which is why so many memory techniques involve forming "mental pictures."

To strengthen our verbal memories, we use rhymes, songs, letter substitutions and other mnemonic gimmicks.

Finally, don't underestimate the importance of kinesthetic memory, or what your *body* remembers. Athletes and dancers certainly don't have to be convinced that the muscles, joints and tendons of their bodies seem to have their own memories. Neither does anyone who's ever remembered a phone number by moving his fingers and "remembering" how it's dialed.

The next time you have to remember a list, any list, say each item out loud and move some part of your body at the same time. A dancer can do the time step and remember her history lecture. A baseball pitcher can associate each movement of his wind up with another item in a list he has to memorize. Even random body movements will do. For example, if you have to memorize a list of countries, just associate each one with a specific movement. For "Burundi," lift your right index finger while saying it. For "Zimbabwe," rotate your neck. Bend a knee for "Equador" and raise your left hand for "San Marino." Kick "Latvia" in the shins and twirl your hair for "Kampuchea." When you have to remember this list of countries, just start moving! It may look a little strange—especially if you make your movements a little too exotic or dramatic in the middle of geography class—but if it works better than anything else for *you*, who cares?

You can also use this new-found memory as a backup to your brain. While you may still memorize key phone numbers, for example, you may also accompany each recitation with the hand movements necessary to actually dial the number. You'll probably find that even if you forget the "mental" tricks you used, your "body memory" will run (or lift or squat or bend or shake!) to the rescue!

Woe unto the poor memorizer

Students, of course, must possess or develop good memories or they risk mediocrity or failure. The mere act of getting by in school means remembering a lot of dates, mathematical and scientific formulas, historical events, characters and plots, sometimes entire poems. (I had a whacko biology teacher who made us memorize the 52 parts of a frog's body. All of which, of course, have been absolutely essential to my subsequent career success. Not.)

Practically, there are two ways of going about this. The most familiar way is rehearsal or repetition. By any name, it is the process of reading or pronouncing something over and over until you've learned it "by heart." (I really didn't want to hold the parts of a frog *too* close to my heart, though.)

But a much easier way—getting back to our computer analogy—is to tag or code things we are trying to remember and to do so with images and words that are either outrageous or very familiar.

For instance, have you ever wondered how, in the days before index cards, ballpoint pens or TelePrompTers, troubadours memorized song cycles and politicians memorized lengthy speeches? Well, in the case of the great Roman orator Cicero, it was a matter of associating the parts of his speeches with the most familiar objects in his life—the rooms of his home. Perhaps the opening of a speech would be linked to his bed chamber, the next part to his yard. As he progressed through the speech, he would, in essence, mentally take his usual morning stroll passing through the rooms of his home.

In other cases, more outrageous associations work much better. The more ridiculous or impossible the association, the more memorable it is. Although absent-mindedness is not one of the problems we will try to solve in this book, a common cure for it illustrates my point.

If you frequently have trouble remembering, say, where you put down your pen, get into the habit of conjuring up some startling image *linking* (a key word later on in this book) the pen and the place. For example, as you're putting your pen down on the kitchen table, think about eating peas off a plate with it or of the pen sticking straight up in a pile of mashed potatoes. Even days later, when you think, "Hmm, where did I leave that ballpoint?" the peas and plate (or mashed potatoes) will come to mind, reminding you of the kitchen table.

The rest is easy

These are the essential principles of memory for which the computer analogy is particularly apt. After all, when dealing with the mind, as with the machine, the GIGO (garbage in, garbage out) rule applies. If you passively allow your brain's process to decide what and how items are stored, you will have a jumbled memory, from which it is difficult to extract even essential bits of knowledge.

On the other hand, if you are selective and careful about assigning useful tags to the items headed for the long-term memory banks, you are on the way to being able to memorize the Manhattan telephone directory!

Chapter 2

And now for a little quiz

I know what you're thinking. You bought this book so you could improve your memory and perform better on exams and those darned pop quizzes, and now I turn around and throw some *more* tests your way. I could note that "them's the breaks!"

Or, as one of my high school teachers used to say, I could encourage you to think of tests as your best friends (no, it wasn't the crazy biology teacher I told you about in Chapter 1). In this book, and throughout your academic career, tests will give you the measure of how far you've come...and how far you've got to go. Follow the advice in this book and your score on similar tests in the last chapter should be 25 percent higher.

Test 1: numbers

Look at the number directly below this paragraph for no more than 10 seconds. Then cover the page (or, better

---

yet, close the book and put it aside) and write down as much of it—in order—as you can.

674216899411539273

Test 2: words and definitions

Below are 15 obscure words along with their definitions. Study this list for 60 seconds. Then cover it up and take the test directly below the list. Allow yourself no more than 90 seconds to complete the quiz...and no peeking.

Dorp	A village.
Ridley	A gray or olive-colored sea turtle.
Afflatus	Inspiration, especially as a result of divine communication.
Baize	A soft feltlike fabric, usually dyed green, commonly used for the tops of game tables.
Wittol	A man who knows of and tolerates his wife's infidelity.
Incult	Rude; unrefined.
Nidation	Implantation of an embryo in the lining of the uterus.
Pecky	(Of timber) Spotted with fungi.
Sclaff	In golf, to scrape the ground with the head of the club just before impact with the ball.
Linguica	A highly spiced Portuguese garlic sausage.
Venatic	Of or pertaining to hunting.
Falcate	Curved like a scythe or sickle; hooked.

Guerdon   A reward; recompense

Kegler   A participant in a bowling game.

Zymurgy   The branch of applied chemistry dealing with fermentation, as in winemaking or brewing.

Have you studied the words diligently? Okay, no cheating now, fill in the blanks:

1. Nobody understood why the_____remained married to his adulterous wife.

2. Winemaking requires a knowledge of_____.

3. _____means "curved."

4. A Portuguese food is_____.

5. Something pertaining to hunting is_____.

6. Another word for rude is_____.

7. Even professional golfers tend to_____.

8. Would you like to be a_____in the bowling match tomorrow?

9. Joe did such a good job on his assignment that his teacher offered him a_____.

10. Which turtle can be gray-colored? _Wittol_.

11. The bark of a log can be_____.

12. The pool table was covered with_____.

13. Nidation occurs where?_____.

14. The worshipper was seeking_____in his time of need.

15. I come from a quiet and traditional_____.

Test 3: names

Take three minutes to memorize the names of the following authors and their Pulitzer Prize-winning books:

Ironweed / William Kennedy
Lonesome Dove / Larry McMurtry
A Thousand Acres / Jane Smiley
The Shipping News / E. Annie Proulx
The Killer Angels / Michael Shaara
Humboldt's Gift / Saul Bellow
The Optimist's Daughter / Eudora Welty
The Fixer / Bernard Malamud
The Executioner's Song / Norman Mailer
Beloved / Toni Morrison
Elbow Room / James Alan McPherson
House Made of Dawn / N. Scott Momaday

Time's up! Okay, cover the list and fill in as many of the blanks as you can. If you get last names only, that's fine. Take another three minutes to complete the quiz:

1. *Lonesome Dove*_____
2. *Ironweed*_____
3. James Alan McPherson_____
4. *A Thousand Acres*_____
5. *House Made of Dawn*_____
6. *The Shipping News*_____
7. Saul Bellow_____
8. *The Fixer*_____
9. *The Killer Angels*_____
10. Eudora Welty_____
11. *The Executioner's Song*_____
12. *Toni Morrison*_____

Test 4: dates

Here are the dates of 12 historical events. Take up to three minutes to memorize them, then cover the page and take the quiz below.

1958   Khrushchev assumed sole power in USSR.

1888   Playwright Maxwell Anderson born.

1940   Arthur Koestler published *Darkness at Noon.*

1977   Republic of Djibouti became independent.

1771   Gustavus III became king of Sweden.

1118   Approximately when Knights Templar order was founded.

1967   Folksinger Woody Guthrie died.

1844   Kierkegaard published *Philosophical Fragments.*

1942   Sir Alexander Korda became first filmmaker ever knighted.

1969   King Idris I overthrown in Libya.

1975   Khalid Ibn Abdul-Aziz acceded to Saudi Arabian throne.

1763   French and Indian Wars ended.

1. Woody Guthrie died in _____.

2. The Republic of _____ became independent in _____.

3. The Knights _____ order was founded around _____.

4. _____ Anderson was born in _____.

5. Khrushchev assumed sole power in the USSR in _____.

6. *Philosophical Fragments* by _____was published in _____.

7. Gustavus III became king of _____in ____.

8. The first filmmaker ever knighted was Sir _____, in _____.

9. The _____and Indian Wars ended in ___.

10. King Idris I was overthrown in _____.

11. Arthur _____published his book in _____.

12. Khalid Ibn _____acceded to the throne in _____.

Test 5: reading retention

Read the text below, then answer the questions following. Give yourself two minutes to read the text and two minutes to answer the questions *without referring back to the paragraph!*

While William Sheridan Allen asserts that only one resident of Norheim in 100 would have joined the Nazi Party if they knew of Hitler's ultimate plans, the National Socialist German Worker's Party nevertheless managed to gain more popular support in the early 1930s than any of the other political parties struggling for power in the turmoil left by World War I.

The social conditions of this period made the people of Norheim, Germany, ready to accept Nazi ideals. By 1930, Norheim was beginning to reel from the growing depression that had blanketed Germany.

The middle class's bank accounts were already nearly wiped out after years of increased taxes, tight credit and mass inflation. Unemployment was increasing every month. Financial dependence on the government was at an all-time high; the government's ability to take care of its citizenry at an all-time low. Norheim and many of the hundreds of other towns and cities just like it were soon ready to follow any leader or party they believed could deliver a dose of economic stability.

The NSDAP, however, faced serious obstacles in its rise to dominance. Neither the Communists (KDP) nor Social Democrats (SPD) were willing to cede their power to the upstart Nazis. But the Nazis skillfully exploited both the biases of the citizenry and the weaknesses of the other parties. Masking their real intentions, the Nazis started slowly, using religion and nationalism to recruit new members. In Norheim, recruiting speeches were often given by local ministers and the Party featured weekly cultural events.

In Norheim, however, the biggest attraction of the upstarts was their anti-Marxist rhetoric; its citizens generally distrusted the SPD because of their "insistent class consciousness." As problems in Russia developed through 1930 and 1931, this distrust only accelerated Norheimers' move to the more radical Nazis.

But no analysis of the rise of Nazism can fail to give large credit to their mastery of propaganda. In this regard, the local party's recruitment methods in Norheim could serve as a paradigm for the rest of Germany. Speeches were always carefully targeted to the particular audience; Nazi leaders had no problems shouting exactly what their listeners wanted to hear. Admission prices to Nazi events were even adjusted according to that particular audience's ability to pay, and small halls were always rented to heighten the illusion that large numbers of people were always in attendance at Nazi events. From 1925 to 1928, for example, the targeted workers heard mainly anti-Semitic propaganda. The middle class in 1929 and the unemployed, Lutherans and small businesspeople added as "targeted classes" in 1930 all received different targeted messages and different treatment. The threat of boycotts, for example, was especially effective with small farmers and businessmen.

Public displays played a major role in convincing the people of Norheim that the NSDAP was the party of the future. Public exhibitions—parades, torchlight processions and open-air speeches (declared illegal by the Prussian government)—made the Nazis seem larger and more popular than they actually were, at least in 1930. Dues-paying members were always significantly outnumbered by supporters, sympathizers and hangers-on, so that the perceived Nazi movement was always far larger than the real one.

Questions

1. The writer's primary purpose in this selection is to:

    A. Describe social conditions in Norheim, Germany.

    B. Explain causes for the rise of Nazism.

    C. Discuss the emphasis of anti-Semitism in Nazi propaganda.

    D. Discuss types of propaganda employed in Europe.

    E. Compare the Social Democrat party to the Nazi party.

2. The author asserts that the Nazis:

A. Worked alongside the other political parties to provide economic stability.

B. Pioneered many social reforms and created jobs.

C. Tried to make themselves seem lesser in number than they were, to promote a feeling of intimacy.

D. Were responsible for the depression after WWI.

E. Were masters of propaganda.

3. Which of the following ideas *cannot* be inferred from the passage?

A. NSDAP are the German initials of the Nazi party.

B. Norheim was in Prussia.

C. Citizens sought religion and nationalism.

D. The Nazi party's exploitation of weaknesses of the other parties caused them to become unpopular.

E. All of the above.

4. The phrase "insistent class consciousness" refers directly to:

A. The KDP.

B. Unemployed businesspeople.

C. The SPD.

D. The NSDAP.

E. Lutherans.

5. The passage states that the Nazi party offered:

A. Weekly cultural events.

B. Decreased taxes.

C. The same type of propaganda to all social classes.

D. Long-established traditions.

E. Financial support.

Here's another chance to test your memory with some recent history, adapted from an article in the January 16, 1996 issue of *The New York Times*:

As Boris Yeltsin seeks to overcome an approval rating that hasn't reached double digits in months and confound countrymen who have declared he has no chance in the June elections, the Communists, sensing a chance for victory in a popular election, have suddenly become courteous and willing to compromise. Since they already dominate the newly-elected Parliament, their aim seems to be to keep the other political parties fighting among themselves, giving them little reason or excuse for establishing an anti-Communist coalition.

Gennadi Seleznyov, Speaker of the Parliament's lower house, or Duma, and a former editor of *Pravda*, looks more like a German banker than an old-style Communist Party apparatchik. That and his poise were two of the reasons he won out over former Central Committee member Valentin Kuptsov in the bid to become spokesperson for the "new and improved" Russian Communists, though the fight for the Speakership was prolonged and nasty.

And the new Speaker has his share of enemies, among them the ultra-nationalist Vladimir Zhirnovsky, who backed the candidate of the nationalist Our Home is Russia centrist party, Ivan Rybkin, in a bid to deny the powerful position to Seleznyov. While repeatedly calling for Yeltsin's resignation, Zhirnovsky has nevertheless supported the perhaps lame duck President on many fronts, including the invasion of Chechnya, the only party in Parliament to do so.

Luckily for Mr. Seleznyov, Grigory A. Yavlinsky, the liberal economist who leads Yablonko, the most reformist party in opposition to Yeltsin, refused to go along with Our Home is Russia and, by extension, Zhirnovsky. By withholding his votes, he assured Seleznyov's victory. While he maintained he held out because he was anti-Communist, it was rumored that, in a mirror of old-style American, back-room politics, he had cut a deal for a couple of much-sought-after committee posts as the price of his votes.

All of this bitter infighting suggests that Seleznyov's gamble might just pay off—it is unlikely that an anti-Communist front will emerge in time for the elections. In addition, the results of the last election must leave him sanguine. Although his party won 149 votes, more than any other (Mr. Zhirinovsky's party was in second place, with 51), in reality the Communists are only a few votes shy of the 226 needed for an outright majority. It turns out that many of the 225 "independent" candidates who ran successfully were not as independent as they had declared—nearly one third of them can be counted on to support Seleznyov's programs.

Such control, unfortunately, tends to indicate that the new Duma will be far less flamboyant and much duller than the old, though undoubtedly more disciplined. And unlike the Speaker, many of the new Communist deputies *are* old-time apparatchiks who are quite accustomed to towing the party line and far less anxious to indulge in free speech.

Questions

6. The author's attitude throughout the passage is:

   A. Supportive of the Communists.
   B. Overly formal toward the reader.
   C. Envious of the Communist party.
   D. Somewhat cynical.
   E. Completely objective.

7. "New and improved" refers to:

   A. Courtesy and willingness to compromise on the part of Russian Communists.
   B. Valentin Kuptsov.
   C. Seleznyov's fight for the Speakership.
   D. The state of affairs in the Duma.
   E. All of the above.

8. The most appropriate title for this passage would be:

   A. "Fight for the Speakership"
   B. "Gennadi Seleznyov—The Man Behind the Myth"
   C. "Odds of June Election In Favor of Communist Party"
   D. "The History of Communism"
   E. "Duma—The Old and New"

9. Using the context of the passage, how would "apparatchiks" be best described?

   A. Radical.
   B. Bold.
   C. Pioneering.
   D. Inexperienced.
   E. Traditional.

10. Which of the following ideas is *not* suggested in the passage?

    A. Vladimir Zhirnovsky is an ultra-nationalist.
    B. Parliament's lower house is also known as Duma.
    C. Ivan Rybkin was the candidate of the Our Home is Russia centrist party.
    D. Boris Yeltsin has had a high approval rating throughout the past few months.
    E. Grigory A. Yavlinsky leads Yablonko.

To check how you did in this last test section, see the answers at the bottom of this page. Go back and check the book itself to figure out the answers to the others.

How did you do?

Take a piece of paper and write down the scores you got on each of these exercises. This will indicate how much improvement you need to successfully recall the material you learn in school. It will also provide a benchmark so that you can see how far you've come when you take similar quizzes in the last chapter.

The emphasis of these tests was not arbitrary. It corresponds exactly with the skills you will be learning throughout this book: memorizing chains of information (such as the book/author and the date/event pairings), developing a sense for numbers, remembering what you read and getting a better grasp on vocabulary.

Answers to Test 5:

1. B	6. D
2. E	7. A
3. D	8. C
4. C	9. E
5. A	10. D

Chapter 3

Roy G. Biv and friends

In Chapter 1 we talked about the need to establish tags or codes for items we wish to remember so that our minds will have relatively little difficulty retrieving them from long-term memory.

In this chapter, we will begin talking about one of the methods used for "tagging" items *before they enter* that morass of memory.

The "chain link" method will help you remember items that appear in sequence, whether it's the association of a date with an event, a scientific term with its meaning or other facts or objects that are supposed to "go together."

The basis for the chain-link system is that memory works best when you associate the unfamiliar with the familiar, though sometimes the association may be very odd. But to really make it effective, the odder the better.

Our boy Roy

One of the simplest methods is to try to remember just the first letter of a sequence. That's how "Roy G. Biv" (the

colors of the spectrum, in order from left to right—red, or-
ange, yellow, green, blue, indigo, violet) got famous. Or
"Every Good Boy Does Fine," to remember the notes on a
musical staff. Or, perhaps the simplest of all, "FACE," to
remember the notes in between. (The latter two work op-
posite of old Roy—using *words* to remember *letters*.) Of
course, not many sequences work out so nicely. If you tried
to memorize the signs of the zodiac with this method,
you'd wind up with (A)ries, (T)aurus, (G)emini, (C)ancer,
(L)eo, (V)irgo, (L)ibra, (S)corpio, (S)agittarius, (C)apricorn,
(A)quarius, (P)isces. Now maybe you can make a name or
a place or something out of ATGCLVLSSCAP, but I can't!

One solution is to make up a simple sentence that uses
the first letters of the list you're trying to remember as the
first letters of each word. For example, "**A T**all **G**iraffe
Chewed **L**eaves **V**ery **L**ow, **S**ome **S**low **C**ows **A**t **P**lay."

Wait a minute! It's the same number of words. Why
not just figure out some way to memorize the first set of
words? What's better about the second set? A couple of
things. First of all, it's easier to picture the giraffe and cow
and what they're doing. As we'll soon see, creating such
mental images is a very powerful way to remember almost
anything. Second, because the words in our sentence bear
some relationship to each other, they're much easier to
remember. Go ahead, try it. See how long it takes you to
memorize the sentence vs. all the signs. This method is
especially easy when you remember some or all of the
items but *don't* remember their *order*.

Remember: Make your sentence(s) memorable to *you*.
Any sentence or series of words that helps you remember
these letters will do. Here are just two more I created in a
few seconds: "**A T**all **G**irl **C**alled **L**ively **V**era **L**oved to **S**ip
Sodas from **C**ans **A**nd **P**lates. **A**ny **T**iny **G**erbil **C**ould **L**ove
Venus. **L**ong **S**illy **S**nakes **C**ould **A**ll **P**ray." Isn't it easy to
make up memorably silly pictures in your head for these?

The rain in Spain

Let's say that I was a literature major who wanted to remember that Vladimir Nabakov published *Lolita,* his most famous novel, in 1958.

The usual way for me to do this would be to repeat over and over again, *"Lolita*, 1958, *Lolita*, 1958..." *ad nauseam*. How much easier it would be to just say, "Lolita was my date in '58"! I've established a link between Lolita, the coquettish girl of Nabakov's novel, the date of publication and some imaginary Saturday night special date. (You'll learn more about how to remember dates in Chapter 8).

In addition, I was able to use another terrific memory technique—rhyming. Rhyme schemes, no matter how silly or banal, can help us remember things for years. For instance, who can forget that it's "*i* before *e* except after *c*, or when it sounds like *a* as in *neighbor* and *weigh*"?

The stranger the better

Let's step away from schoolwork for a moment to consider the case of a woman who can't remember where she puts anything—car keys, wallet, her month-old baby (just kidding!).

Using the chain-link method would ensure that she would never forget. For instance, let's say she puts her car keys down on her kitchen counter and, as she does, thinks of a car plowing right into the kitchen and through the countertop. Will that woman be able to forget what she did with her keys? Would you?

Or, to pick an example more germane to academic life, let's say that you wanted to remember that *mitosis* is the process whereby one cell divides itself into two. Instead of repeating word and definition countless times, why not think, "My toes is dividing," and form a mental picture of two of your toes separating? Much easier, isn't it?

Where in the world is...?

The best way to teach this technique is by example, so let's take another one. Suppose you wanted to remember the following list of 10 relatively obscure world capitals (and, of course, the countries they go with): Tirana (Algeria), Belmopan (Belize), Thimphu (Bhutan), Suva (Fiji), Brazzaville (Congo), Moroni (The Comoros), Accra (Ghana), Muscat (Oman), Valletta (Malta), Funafuti (Tuvalu).

Study the list for no more than two minutes, cover up the page, and try to write down as many combinations as you remember. Heck, you don't even have to do them in order (but you get serious extra credit if you do!).

Time's up

How did you do? Did you get them all right? How long do you think you'd have to study this list to be able to recite it perfectly? I guarantee you it would take a lot less time if you established a chain link that you could just reel in out of your memory bank.

Here are the associations and pictures I would use to remember this list (and remember, make your pictures memorable to *you*!):

Tirana (Algeria): Being a New Yorker, the thing that immediately came to mind was the *Tawana* Brawley case in which Rev. *Al* Sharpton was involved. I'd remember a picture of the Reverend being *jeered* when it was discovered the whole thing was a hoax.

Belmopan (Belize): Picture *Elmo* from "Sesame Street" wearing a big *B* on his chest (hence *Belmo*) while holding a pan and begging you to take it (*Puleeze!*).

Thimphu (Bhutan): Thimphu is a *thimble* trying on a *tan boot*. Picture it on the pan Elmo is holding to make it really memorable!

Suva (Fiji): I'd remember the Indian god *Siva* being very nervous (*fidgeting*).

Brazzaville (Congo): So happens I once worked with an author named Jerry *Braza*. I'd picture him in his *villa* playing his *bongo*.

Moroni (The Comoros): The *Commodores* (an old singing group for those of you under 20!) eating *macaroni*.

Accra (Ghana): "The water (*agua*) is *gone*."

Muscat (Oman): *Muskrat! Oh, my!* You can always combine these last two, picturing yourself looking for water, finding none, then seeing a fat muskrat grinning with water rolling down his cheeks. (Remember, I *said* strange.)

Valetta (Malta)—To make it really weird, the muskrat's *valet, Walter* is standing at attention, waiting to dress him. (See the next one; it's gets better.)

Funafuti (Tuvalu)—That's right, he's dressing him in that *fun* and *fruity* vest from *True Value* hardware stores!

Got all that? Okay, let's put it all together into a single string. Now it really gets strange:

So you're standing on a street corner watching Reverend Al getting jeered while he talks about Tawana. Elmo runs in front of him, carrying a pan that holds a thimble trying on a tan boot. To the right, there's Siva fidgeting in front of Jerry Braza's villa, where he's playing the bongos to accompany the Commodores while they sing and eat macaroni. (This has all made me very thirsty, so...) I look for some water, only to find it's gone. The muskrat drank it. And there he is (oh my!) while his valet, Walter, stands by, waiting to dress him in his fun and fruity vest from True Value.

Is this efficient?

You're probably wondering just how much time it took me to construct these ridiculous associations and the even more bizarre story to go with them. The answer: about three minutes. I'll bet it will take you a lot longer to memorize the list of capitals and countries. And my way of doing this is so much more fun! Not only that, but I'd be willing to bet that you'll remember "that muskrat and his valet" a lot longer than "Muscat" and "Valetta."

The reason is that you use so much more of your brain when you employ techniques like this. Reciting a list of facts over and over to yourself uses only three of your faculties—sight (as you read them from the page), speech and hearing—in carving the memory trail. Constructing a bizarre story like the one we just did also puts to work your imagination, perhaps the most powerful of your mind's many powers.

How the French do it

Let's try another example, one with which I doubt you are at all familiar—the French Revolutionary calendar: Brumaire, Floréal, Frimaire, Fructidore, Germinal, Messidor, Nivôse, Pluviôse, Prairiel, Thermidor, Vendémiaire, Ventôse.

Here's the way I would remember: There'd be a big *broom* sweeping through the *air* across a field of *flowers*. That's the first picture—two down (Brumaire, Floréal).

Now the broom would turn into a *frying pan* flying through the *air* (Frimaire).

Suddenly a refrigerator (naturally a Frigidaire) would open (Fructidore) and out would pop my friends Germ and Al (Germinal). They'd yell at me, "Hey, why have you got such a *messy door*?" (Messidor).

Well, people yelling at me make me *nervous* (Nivôse) so I'd stammer, "*Pl*ease, *you've toas*ted me!" (Pluviôse).

So I got down on some *rail*road tracks to *pray* (Prairiel) until a giant Lobster *Thermidor* came tumbling down in a *vend*ing machine, right out of the *air* (Vendémiaire).

The smell went right to my nose (Ventôse).

Immediately after making up this story, I turned away from the computer and, without even trying, recited the words I was supposed to have just memorized. It's actually that easy.

Now you try. How would you remember another obscure list, like this longer one of alphabets? Chalcidan, cuneiform, Cyrillic, devanagari, entrangelo, futhark, Glagol, Glossic, Greek, Gurmukhi, hieroglyphs, hiragana, ideograph, kana, katakanam Kuffic, linear A, linear B, logograph, nagari, naskhi, ogham, pictograph, Roman, runic, syllabary.

Time yourself. When you can construct a series of pictures to remember a list like this—and remember it—all in less than five minutes, you are well on your way to mastering this powerful memory technique.

Hear my song

Observations of people who have been in accidents or suffered other types of severe brain trauma have yielded many interesting insights into the ways our minds and memories work. For instance, people who have had the left side of their brains damaged might lose their ability to speak and remember words and facts, but often are still able to sing songs perfectly.

Current thinking on this is that the faculty for speech resides in the left hemisphere of the brain, while the ability to sing can be found in the right.

Since it is my feeling that the more of your mind's power you put behind the job of remembering, the better you'll do, I'd like to suggest song as another great way to remember strings of information.

For instance, I remember few things from chemistry class in my junior year of high school (not having had memory training at that time). But one thing I'll never forget is that ionization is a dissociative reaction; it is the result of electrons becoming separated from their nuclei.

The reason I remember this is that Mr. Scott, my crazy chemistry teacher, came into class singing (to the main theme from the opera "Grenada") "I-, I-, I-onization. I-, I-, I-onization. Oh, this is, oh, this is a dissociative reaction in chemistry."

Or, there's the case of one of Robert Frost's most loved poems, "Stopping by Woods On a Snowy Evening." Did you ever realize that you could sing the entire poem to the music of "Hernando's Hideaway" by Xavier Cugat?

Try it with the last four lines—"The woods are lovely dark and deep, but I have promises to keep, and miles to go before I sleep. And miles to go before I sleep." Trust me: it works for the whole poem. Unfortunately, that beautiful poem, one of my favorites, may now be ruined forever!

Just do it

Music is one of the ways that you can create a chain link to improve your memory. As the examples we've already discussed show, there are many others:

Unusual. To the extent possible, make the chain-link scenarios you construct highly unusual.

Active. Don't think of an object just sitting there. Have it do something! Remember Mom and her car smashing through the kitchen counter earlier in the chapter? How can such an image be forgotten?

Emotional. Conjure up a scenario in establishing your chain link that elicits an emotional reaction—joy, sorrow, physical pain, whatever.

Rhyming. Many lessons for preschoolers and those just in first and second grade are done with rhymes. If it works for them, it should work for you, right?

Acronyms. If you've taken trigonometry, you've probably come across good old Chief *SOH-CAH-TOA.* If you've been lucky enough to evade trig (or didn't have Mr. Oldehoff in 7th Grade), you've missed one of the easiest way to remember trigonometric functions: *S*ine equals *O*pposite/ *H*ypotenuse; *C*osine equals *A*djacent/*H*ypotenuse; *T*angent equals *O*pposite/*A*djacent.

Relax and have fun

You're probably thinking that all of this doesn't sound like it will make your life any easier. I know it *seems* like a lot of work to think of the soundalikes and construct crazy scenarios or songs using them. Trust me: If you start applying these tips *routinely*, they will quickly become second nature and make you a more efficient student.

There's the rub

The only problem with this method is that you might occasionally have trouble remembering what your soundalike signified in the first place. But the process of forming the link will, more often than not, obviate the problem because the link to the original item is made stronger by the act of forming these crazy associations. Again, the crazier they are, the more *memorable* they are.

In the next chapter, we'll get away from straight factual memory for a little while and talk about how we can get a better grasp of material as we read through it the first time.

Chapter 4

Reading and remembering

Nothing you do as you pursue your studies *in any subject* will serve you as well as learning to read...and remembering what you've read, whenever you need to. The ability to recall a great amount of detail *without* having to review is a tremendous benefit to *any* student.

In college, where the reading demands of a *single* course can be voluminous, just think how much more students could get out of texts and how much more efficiently they could prepare for exams and term papers *if* they could get most of the information they need *the first time around!*

This chapter will show you how to do it...easily.

Reading to remember

The best way to begin any reading assignment is to skim the pages to get an overall view of what information is included in the text. Then, scan and highlight the text and/or take notes in your notebook.

I'm going to digress for a moment, taking your side, to criticize a large number, perhaps even the majority, of the texts you're forced to plow through. This criticism is constructive: I want to show you the deficiencies in textbooks that you will have to overcome in order to be the best student you can be *without unnecessary effort.*

Think of the differences in writing and presentation between newspapers and textbooks. Newspapers are edited and designed to make reading simple. Most newspaper articles are organized using the "pyramid" approach: The first paragraph (the top of the pyramid) makes the major point of the story, then successive paragraphs add more detail and make related points, filling out the pyramid. You can get a pretty good handle on the day's news by reading the headlines and the first few paragraphs of each story. If you're interested in more details, just read on.

Textbooks, on the other hand, usually are *not* written to allow for such an approach. Many times authors begin with a relatively general introduction to the material, and then lead readers through their reasoning to major points.

The next time you have to read a history, geography or similar text, try skimming the assigned pages first. Read the heads, subheads and callouts, those brief notes or headings in the outside margins of each page that summarize the topic covered in the section. Read the first sentence of each paragraph. Then go back and read the details.

To summarize the skimming process:

1. Read and be sure you understand the title or heading. Try rephrasing it as a question for further clarification of what you read.
2. Examine all the subheadings, illustrations and graphics—these will all help you identify the significant matter within the text.

3. Read thoroughly the introductory paragraphs, the chapter summary and any questions at the chapter's end.

4. Read the first sentence of every paragraph—this generally includes the main idea.

5. Evaluate what you have gained from this process: Can you answer the questions at the end of the chapter? Could you intelligently participate in a class discussion of the material?

6. Write a brief summary that capsulizes what you have learned from your skimming.

7. Based on this evaluation, decide whether a more thorough reading is required.

I've found that the most effective way to read a textbook is to first go through reading the headlines, subheadings and the callouts so that I know the major points of the chapter *before* I get to them. Then I'm more attuned to absorb when I arrive at these sections. In other words, by the time I get to the material for which I am reading the chapter, my antennae are up and my mind is ready to soak everything up.

Reading faster without speed reading

While the heads, subheads, first sentences and other author-provided hints will help you get a quick read on what a chapter's about, some of the *words* in that chapter will help you concentrate on the important points and ignore the unimportant. Knowing when to speed up, slow down, ignore or really concentrate will help you read both faster *and* more effectively.

When you see words like "likewise," "moreover," "also," "furthermore" and the like, you should know nothing new is being introduced. If you already know what's going on, speed up or skip what's coming entirely.

On the other hand, when you see words like "on the other hand," "nevertheless," "however," "rather," "but" and their ilk, it's time to slow down—you're getting information that certainly adds a new perspective—it may even contradict what you've just read.

Watch out for "payoff" words such as, "in conclusion," "therefore," "thus," "consequently," "to summarize"— especially if you only have time to "hit the high points" of a chapter or if you're reviewing for a test. Here's where the real meat is, where everything that went before is happily tied up in a nice fat bow, a present that enables you to avoid having to unwrap the entire chapter.

One chapter at a time

Sometimes students have a desire to rush through the reading of textbooks to "get it over with." Granted, there are textbook writers who seem to go out of their way to encourage such a reaction. Don't fall into the trap.

Instead, before getting to the next chapter as rapidly as possible, stop to perform the following exercise:

- Write down definitions of any key terms you think are essential to *understanding* the topic.
- Write down questions and answers that you think help *clarify* the topic. Play teacher for a minute and design a "pop" quiz on the chapter.
- Write questions for which you *don't have the answers*, then go back and find them by rereading the chapter, noting questions you'd like to ask the professor or answer through further reading.

When reading is a formula

Texts for mathematics, economics and science require a slightly different treatment. You should follow the steps outlined above, but with one important addition: Make sure that you thoroughly understand the concepts expressed in the various charts and graphs and do *not* move on to the next section unless you have mastered the previous one.

You must understand one section before moving on to the next, since the next concept is usually *based* on the previous one. If there are sample problems, solve those that tie in with the section you have just read to make sure that you understand the concepts imparted. If you still fail to grasp a key concept or equation, start again and try again. But *don't* move on—you'll just be wasting your time.

These texts require such a slow, steady approach, even one with a lot of backtracking or, for that matter, a lot of wrong turns. "Trial and error" *is* an accepted method of scientific research. The key, though, is to make it *informed* trial and error—having a clear idea of where you're heading and *learning* from each error. While trial and error is okay, it is much more important to be able to easily apply the same analysis (solution, reasoning) to a slightly different problem, which requires real understanding. Getting the right answer just because you eliminated every *wrong* one may be a very viable strategy for taking a test, but it's a lousy way to assure yourself you've actually learned something.

Understanding is especially essential in any technical subject. It's easy for some of you to do well on math tests because you have a great memory, are lucky or have an innate math "sense." Trust me, sooner or later your luck runs out, your memory overloads and your calculations become "sense"-less. You *will* reach a point where, without understanding, you will be left confused on the shore, watching your colleagues sail heroically to the promised land.

Whether math and science come easily to you or make you want to find the nearest pencil-pocketed computer nerd and throttle him, there are some ways you can do better at such technical subjects, without the world's greatest memory, a lot of luck or any "radar":

- Whenever you are able, "translate" formulas and numbers into words. To test your understanding, try to put your translation into *different* words.

- Even if you're not a particularly visual person, pictures can often help. Try translating a particularly vexing math problem into a drawing or diagram.

- Before you even get down to solving a problem, is there any way for you to estimate the answer or, at least, the range within which the answer should fall (greater than one, but less than 10)? This is the easy way to make sure you wind up in the right ballpark.

- Play around. There are often different paths to the same solution or even equally valid solutions. If you find one, try to find others. This is a great way to increase your understanding of all the principles involved.

- When you are checking your calculations, try working backwards. I've found it an easier way to catch simple mathematical errors.

- Try to figure out what is being asked, what principles are involved, what information is important, what's not. I can't resist an example here: A plane crashed in the mountains right on the Canadian-U.S. border. After it stopped sliding, approximately one half of the now broken jet was in each country. The plane was 424 feet long and 38 feet wide, with a wingspan of 284 feet. It landed at a speed of 47 knots and traveled 4,290 meters before it came to a complete stop. The passengers consisted of 47 women, 142 men and 38 children. The flight crew was 4 men and 6 women. A careful inventory showed the plane broke into 147 various pieces, 67 percent of which were in the U.S.

  Think you've got it all? Here's the question: In which country were the survivors buried?

- Teach someone else. Trying to explain mathematical concepts to someone else will quickly pinpoint what you really know or don't know. It's virtually impossible to get someone *else*—especially someone who is slower than you at all this stuff—to understand the material if *you* don't.

By the way, the answer is,"You don't bury *survivors!*" In case you didn't notice, *none* of the mathematical information given had the slightest bearing on the answer.

You should approach foreign language texts the same way, especially basic texts that teach vocabulary (we'll deal with memorizing vocabulary words in the next chapter) and fundamental rules of grammar. If you haven't mastered the words you're supposed to in the first section, you'll have trouble reading the story at the end of the third.

Follow the yellow brick road

When I discovered highlighters during my first year of college, my reaction was, "Where have you been all my life?" I couldn't believe how terrific they were for zeroing in on the really important material in a text. However, I soon realized that I was highlighting *too much*—rereading highlighted sections became nearly the same as reading the whole darn text again.

I developed this set of rules for making the most of my highlighters during college, when my work load became much heavier:

1. I highlighted areas of the text with which I didn't feel completely comfortable.
2. I identified single words and sentences that encapsulated a section's major ideas and themes.
3. I underlined to make studying easier. I concentrated on the key words, facts and concepts, and skipped the digressions, multiple examples and unnecessary explanations.
4. I underlined my classroom notes as well as texts to make studying from *them* easier.

To sharpen your underlining skills, read through the next three paragraphs and indicate with your highlighter the key sentence(s) or words:

When told to communicate, most people immediately think of writing or speaking. Yet, there is another form of communication that everyone uses—without realizing it. Through various facial expressions, body movements and gestures, we all have a system of nonverbal communication.

We constantly signal to others our feelings and attitudes unconsciously through actions we may not even realize we are performing. One type is called barrier signals. Since most people usually feel safer behind a barrier, they often unthinkingly fold their arms or find some other pretext for placing their arms in front of their body when they feel insecure.

Such nonverbal communication can lead to serious misunderstanding if you are not careful. Take the simple symbol you make by forming a circle with your thumb and forefinger. In America it means "Okay." In France, however, it signifies a zero, something—or someone—worthless. Imagine the offense a French waiter might take if you signified your satisfaction with your meal with this sign! You would offend and insult when you intended to praise.

Which of these sentences will you underline? I'd probably underline "nonverbal communication," "barrier signals," and "insecure" (with an arrow drawn to "barrier signals" to remind me of the reason they're used).

And I would probably underline the first sentence in the second paragraph, which summarizes the point of the article.

Do you think you would underline anything in the third paragraph? Why wouldn't you? It's an example—a nice one, a simple one, an understandable one—but if you understand the concept, you really don't need anything else.

If you had to review the text for an exam, you would glance at the one sentence and four or five words you highlighted to get the gist of the three paragraphs. This will save you a tremendous amount of time.

Retention

The word "retention" is frequently mentioned alongside "reading."

Retention is the process by which we keep imprints of past experiences in our minds, the "storage depot." Subject to other actions of the mind, what is retained can be recalled when needed. Items are retained in the same order in which they are learned. So, your studying should build one fact, one idea, one concept on another.

Broad concepts can be retained much more easily than details. Master the generalities and the details will fall into place.

If you think something is important, you will retain it more easily. An attitude that says, "I *will* retain this," *will* help you remember. So, convincing yourself that what you are studying is something you *must* retain and recall *increases* your chance of adding it to your long-term memory bank.

As I mentioned in the last chapter, let yourself react to the data you are reading. Associating new information with what you already know will make it easier to recall.

Still having trouble?

If you follow these suggestions and are still having trouble retaining what you read, try these other ideas. They are a bit more time-consuming, but undoubtedly will help you.

Take notes

Do you own the book you're reading? Do you not care about preserving it for posterity? Then use its margins for notes. Go beyond mere highlighting to assign some ranking to the facts conveyed by the text.

I used to use a little shorthand method to help me remember written materials. I'd draw vertical lines close to the text to assign levels of importance. One vertical line meant that the material should be reviewed; two indicated that the facts were very important; asterisks would signify "learn or fail" material. I'd insert question marks for material that I wanted one of my more intelligent friends or the teacher to explain to me further. I'd use circles to indicate the information I was dead sure would show up on the next test.

Interestingly, I found that the very act of assigning relative weights of importance to the text and keeping a lookout for test material helped me remember because it heightened my attention. (For a more detailed method of taking notes, see Chapter 6.)

Become an active reader

Earlier in this chapter, I urged you to quiz yourself on written material to ascertain how well you'd retained it. If this doesn't work, try asking the questions *before* you read the material.

For instance, even though I have been an avid reader throughout much of my academic life, I had some trouble with the reading comprehension sections of standardized tests the first couple of times I attempted them. Why? I think I had a tendency to rush through these sections.

Then, someone suggested to me that I read the questions *before* I read the passage. And presto! Great scores in reading comp! (765 points on my verbal SAT for all of you doubters.)

While you won't always have such a ready-made list of questions, there are other sources—the summaries at the beginnings of chapters, the synopses in tables of contents. Pay attention to these.

For instance, if an author states in an introductory paragraph, "Containing the Unsatisfactory Result of Oliver's Adventure; and a Conversation of Some Importance between Harry Maylie and Rose," as Charles Dickens does in *Oliver Twist*, you may ask yourself:

- What was Oliver's unsatisfactory adventure?
- What could the result of it have been?
- What could Harry and Rose be talking about that's so important?

Believe it or not, this technique will train your mind to hone in on those important details when they arise in the story. It would also be a good idea to ask yourself these questions immediately after you finish the chapter. It will help you ascertain whether you "got" the important points of the chapter and help you retain the information longer.

Understand, don't memorize

Approach any text with the intent of *understanding* it rather than memorizing it. Understanding is a key part of memorization. Don't stop the flow of information during your reading (other than to underline and note). Go back and memorize later.

Organize the material

Our minds crave order. Optical illusions work because the mind is bent on imposing order on every piece of information coming in from the senses. As you read, think of ways to organize the material to help your mind absorb it.

I always liked diagrams with single words and short phrases connected with arrows to show cause and effect relationships. Or I would highlight in texts the *reasons* things occurred with a special mark (I used a triangle).

Develop good reading habits

It's impossible for anyone to remember what they've read at 3 a.m., or while they were waiting to go on the biggest date of their lives. Set aside quiet time when you're at your best. Are you a morning person? Then wake up early to do your reading. Do you get going at 6 p.m.? Then, get your reading done before stopping by the rathskeller.

Don't forget to use your dictionary to look up terms you don't understand. (Or put the information in the next chapter to use. Then you won't need a dictionary!)

On we go

Each time you attempt to read something that you must recall, use this six-step process to assure you'll remember:

1. **Evaluate the material.** Define your purpose for reading. Identify your interest level and get a sense of how difficult the material is.

2. **Choose appropriate reading techniques** for the purpose of your reading. If you are reading to grasp the main idea, then that is exactly what you will recall.

3. **Identify the important facts** and remember what you need to. Let your purpose for reading dictate what you remember, and identify associations that connect the details to recall.

4. **Take notes.** Use your own words to give a synopsis of the main ideas. Use an outline, diagram or concept tree to show relationship or pattern. Your notes serve as an important backup to your memory. Writing down key points will further reinforce your ability to remember.

5. **Review.** Quiz yourself on those things you *must* remember. Develop some system by which you review notes at least three times before you are required to recall. The first review should be shortly after you have read, the second should come a few days later and the final review should take place just before you are expected to recall. This process will help you avoid cram sessions.

6. **Implement.** Find opportunities to *use* the knowledge you have gained. Study groups and class discussions are invaluable opportunities to put what you have learned to good use. Participate in group discussions—they'll greatly increase what you recall.

If you find after all this work that you need still *more* help with reading, comprehension and recall, I recommend *Improve Your Reading,* one of the other volumes in my *How to Study Program.*

Chapter 5

One chapter to a better vocabulary

William F. Buckley, watch out.

The whole demeanor of Mr. Buckley, star moderator of "Firing Line"—all pursed lips and raised eyebrows—implies that becoming a master of vocabulary is more difficult than it actually is. (Unless, of course, you currently attend or graduated from Yale, in which case it may well *be* a difficult task—at least, that's one Princetonian's erudite opinion.)

No, the way to a great vocabulary is at your fingertips, and it has absolutely nothing to do with those Word-A-Day calendars.

In this chapter, I will show you two ways to improve your memory for sesquipedalian (having many syllables) and small, obscure words.

The building blocks method

Whenever possible, try to remember *concepts* rather than memorizing random data. For instance, if someone told you to memorize a long string of numbers—e.g., 147101316192225—it would be far better to note that each number is three higher than the one before and simply remember that rule.

Similarly, it is far better to absorb the way words are constructed, to memorize a relatively small number of prefixes, suffixes and roots, rather than trying to cram the contents of *Webster's Dictionary* into your already crowded memory.

A note on English

Our borrowed mother tongue, English, is perhaps the most democratic of all languages. Built on a Celtic base, it has freely admitted a multitude of words from other languages, particularly French, Latin, Greek, German and a rich body of slang (from anywhere we could get it).

The oldest branches in this diverse family tree, Celtic and Old English, are the least amenable to some of the techniques we are about to learn. These are basically simple words, not built in complicated fashion as are Latinate and Greek terms.

However, as any crossword puzzle addict can tell you, our language is replete with myriad Romance words (those from French, Italian and Spanish) that often can be dissected into rather simple elements.

The roots of language

Here are two dozen or so roots from Latin and Greek that contribute to thousands of English words:

Root	Meaning	Example
annu	year	annual
aqua	water	aquarium
arch	chief	archenemy
bio	life	biology
cap, capt	take, seize	capture
chron	time	chronological
dic, dict	say	indicate
duc, duct	lead	induction
fact, fect	do, make	effective
fer	carry, bear	infer
graph	write	graphics
homo	same, identical	homonym
logos	word	logical
manu	hand	manufacture
mitt, miss	send	remittance
path	feel, feeling	apathy
ped, pod	foot	pedal
plico	fold	implication
pon, posit	place, put	imposition
port	carry	export
psyche	mind	psychopathic
scrib	write	scribe
spec	observe, see	speculative
tend, tent	stretch	intention
tene,	have, hold	tenacious
vert, vers	turn	introverted

The cart before the horse

As the above examples suggest, knowing the definition of a root alone is usually not enough. Prefixes, the fragments added to the beginning of a word, can greatly change the message conveyed by the root. Here are some examples of common prefixes:

Prefix	Meaning	Example
a-, ab-	from, away	aberration
a-, an-	without, not	amoral
ad-, af-, at-, ag-	to, toward	admonition
		affection
		aggressor
ant-, anti-	against	antidote
ante-	before	antecedent
bi-	two	bicycle
con-, com-	with, together	commitment
de-	away from	deviant
dis-	apart, opposite	disrespect
e-, ex-	out of, over	exorbitant
en-	in	envelope
extra-	beyond	extraordinary
hyper-	above, over	hyperthermia
hypo-	under	hypoglycemic
il-, im-, in-	not	illicit
		impeccable
inter-	between	intercept
intra-	within	intrauterine
mal-	evil	maladjusted
multi-	many	multiply

ob-, op-	toward, against	obdurate, opposite
per-	through	perspicacious
peri-	around	peripatetic
post-	after	posthumous
pre-	before	premonition
pro-	for, forth	production
re-	again, back	regression
sub-, sup-	under	substantiate
sym-, syn-	with, together	sympathetic synergy
tri-	three	triangle
un-	not	uncool

The tail that wags the dog

The last, but certainly not the least important building block of words is the suffix, which quite often indicates how the word is being used. Suffixes can be used to turn an adjective into an adverb (the "-ly" ending), to compare things (smallER, smallEST) or even to modify other suffixes (liveLIEST). Some suffixes with which you should be familiar are:

Suffix	Meaning	Example
-able, -ible	capable of	pliable
-ac, -al, -ial	pertaining to	hypochondriac remedial
-acy	quality of	fallacy, legacy
-age	quality of	outage
-ance, -ence	state of being	abundance
-ant, -ent	one who...	student

-ary	devoted to	secretary
-cy	state of	lunacy
-dom	quality of, state of	martyrdom kingdom
-en	made of	wooden
-er, -or	one who...	perpetrator
-ful	full of	woeful
-hood	state of	neighborhood
-ic	pertaining to	pedantic
-ine	like	leonine
-ion	act of	extermination
-ish, -ity	quality of	purplish, enmity
-ist	one who practices	novelist
-ive	disposition of	active
-less	lacking	penniless
-ly	like	cowardly
-ment	process of	enlightenment
-ness	state of	holiness
-ory	pertaining to	memory
-ose	full of	grandiose
-ous	like	porous
-ry	state of	ribaldry
-some	full of	toothsome

Practice those prefixes

Of course, I don't expect that you'll memorize these lists. But if you read them over a few times, paying particular attention to the examples, you'll absorb the roots, prefixes and suffixes fairly quickly.

Here's a list of 20 words. Write the definition in the blank space using what you remember of the building blocks of words above. Then, check to see how you did using the lists above.

1. Perspicacious _____
2. Psychographic _____
3. Introspective _____
4. Subjudice _____
5. Contentious _____
6. Transponder _____
7. Complected _____
8. Contravene _____
9. Presentiment _____
10. Ductile _____
11. Neologism _____
12. Implicit _____
13. Replicate _____
14. Subtend _____
15. Intermittent _____
16. Transubstantiate _____
17. Conurbation _____
18. Hyperthermia _____
19. Realottment_____
20. Antipathy _____

Method with madness in it

How did you do on the quiz? I'll bet a lot better than you thought, simply because of this rather brief introduction to etymology.

Now let's examine another way of remembering so that you can have powerful words at your disposal—the soundalike method. As we saw in Chapter 3, forming your own associations—sometimes wildly outrageous ones—can be quite helpful in carving easy-access roads to the long-term memory banks.

In order to use this method, create a scenario using the soundalike of the word or parts of the word and the definition of the word.

Consider this example: Let's say that you've seen the word "ostracize" countless times, but can never quite remember that it means "to cast out from a group." You could then create this nonsense thought: "The ostrich's eyes are so big, no one wants to look at him."

In such an example, you would be using the size of the ostrich and creating an absurd reason he might be a cast out. Or, I could have made the phrase: "The ostrich's size was so big he was thrown out of his hole."

Sure, you're saying, that's an easy example. But let's take another one. Since we're in a chapter on vocabulary, let's consider "sesquipedalian," which means "having many syllables" or "tending to use long words." Our soundalike association could be: "She says quit peddling those big words."

Or, one picture might be worthy of a particular vocabulary word. You might associate the difficult-to-remember word not with a phrase, but with an outrageous picture.

For instance, to remember that the word "flambe" means a food covered with flames, think of a plate of food with bees whose wings are ablaze flying from it.

Again, as we learned in Chapter 3, this sort of exercise is not a lot of work, but it is a great deal of fun. It'll help your mind hold onto words, even those you use infrequently, forever.

Here's a list of "50-cent words" with soundalikes that will make them easy to learn:

Cutaneous (pertaining to or affecting the skin): "Cute skin, ain't it just?"

Necromancy (a method of divination through invocation of the dead): "Nancy, dig up Phil Niekro."

Hoosegow (slang for a jail): "Who's cow is in jail?"

Welter (to toss or heave): "Toss it here, Walter!"

Sullage (sewage or waste): "Sully, age is a waste."

Hieromonk (an Eastern monk who was also a priest): "Need a priest? Hire a monk."

Avouch (to declare or assert): " 'Ouch!' he vowed."

Cognomen (a nickname or epithet): "No man was named Cog."

Dikdik (a tiny antelope): "Did did you you see see that that antelope antelope?"

Guayabera (a kind of Cuban sport skirt or jacket): "Put on your shirt and buy me a beer, Fidel."

Liatigo (strap on a Western saddle): "Let that strap go, horsey!"

Petiole (the stalk by which a leaf is attached to a stem): "Pet my old leaf?"

Mizzle (to rain in fine drops): "It's drizzling, Ma."

Jaguarundi (a tropical American wildcat): "Help! There's Jaguar undies on top!"

Frutescent (shrubby): "Smelly fruits grew on the shrub."

Refrangible (capable of being refracted, like rays of light): "Hey, Ray, ball the light for Angie."

Osteophyte (an abnormal outgrowth of bone): "Two bones were fighting, Ossie."

Icosahedron (a solid having 20 faces): "I guess he'd run 20."

Euclase (rare green or blue mineral): "That green gem you got sure is classy."

With this tool, you can become a horribly pedantic conversationalist and never have to run to the dictionary while you're reading *Finnegan's Wake.*

Try a sample

Still another method that works quite well—and is relatively easy to employ for some words—is to associate a word with a very particular example. If you're reading an English grammar textbook and you come across the term "oxymoron," which is defined as "a figure of speech combining seemingly contradictory words or phrases," think how much easier it would be to remember if your notes looked like this:

Oxymoron	jumbo shrimp, cruel kindness
Onomatopoeia	PLOP, PLOP, FIZZ, FIZZ
Metaphor	food for thought
Simile	this is *like* that

Chapter 6

Taking notes to remember texts

I have a confession to make, a rather difficult one for someone whose specialty is careers and education: To this very day, I resent having to write an outline for a book, article or research project. I'd much rather just sit down and start writing.

I would have hated myself in school if I knew then what I know now: You should do outlines while you are *reading,* as well. The fact is, outlines will help you review a text more quickly and remember it more clearly.

In Chapter 4, we advised using highlighters to, well, highlight important messages. This is great in a relatively easy-to-remember text. For other courses, it would be a sure sign of masochism, as it assures only one thing: You will have to read a great deal of your deadly textbooks all over again when exam time rolls around.

Likewise, marginalia usually make the most sense only in context, so the messy method of writing small notes in white space around the text will engender a great deal of rereading as well.

So then, what's *the* most effective way to read and remember your textbooks? *Sigh.* Yes, that good old outline.

Reverse engineering

Outlining a textbook, article or other secondary source is a little bit like Japanese "reverse engineering"—a way of developing a schematic for something so that you can see exactly how it's been put together. Seeing that logic of construction will help you a great deal in remembering the book—by putting the author's points down in *your* words, you will be building a way to retrieve the key points of the book more easily from your memory.

Outlining will force you to distinguish the most important points from those of secondary importance, helping you build a true understanding of the topic.

The bare bones of outlining

Standard outlines use Roman numerals, (I, II, III, etc.), capital letters, Arabic numerals (1, 2, 3, 4, etc.), and lower-case letters and indentations to show the relationships between and importance of topics in the text. While you certainly don't have to use the Roman-numeral system, your outline would be organized in the following manner:

Title
Author

I. First importar.t topic in the text
  A. First subtopic
    1. First subtopic of A
      a. First subtopic of 1
      b. Second subtopic of 1
    2. Second subtopic of A
II. The second important topic in the text

Get the idea? In a book, the Roman numerals usually would refer to chapters; the capital letters to subheadings and the Arabic numbers and lower-case letters to blocks of paragraphs. In an article or single chapter, the Roman numerals would correspond to subheadings, capital letters to blocks of paragraphs, Arabic numbers to paragraphs, small letters to key sentences.

What's he getting at?

We understand things in outline form. Ask an intelligent person to recount something and he'll state the main points and only enough details to make his words interesting and understandable. The discipline of creating outlines will help you zero in on the most important points an author is making and capture them, process them and, thereby, retain them.

Sometimes an author will have the major point of a paragraph in the first sentence. But just as often, the main idea of a paragraph or section will follow some of these telltale words: therefore, because, thus, since, as a result.

When you see any of these words, you should identify the material they introduce as the major points in your outline. Material immediately preceding and following almost always will be in support of these major points.

Create a time line

I always found it frustrating to read textbooks in social studies. I'd go through chapters on France, England, the Far East, and have a fairly good understanding of those areas, but have no idea where certain events stood in a global context. As more and more colleges add multicultural curricula, you may find it even more difficult to "connect" events in 17th-century France or 19th-century

Africa with what was happening in the rest of the world (let alone the U.S.).

An excellent tool for overcoming that difficulty is a time line that you can update periodically. It will help you visualize the chronology and remember the relationship of key world events.

For instance, a simple, abridged time line of Charles Dickens's literary life would look like this (I would suggest you create a horizontal time line, but the layout of this book makes reproducing it that way difficult. So here's a vertical version.):

1812	Birth
1836	First book published (*Sketches by Boz*)
1837	*Pickwick Papers*
1838	*Oliver Twist*
1850	*David Copperfield*
1853	*Bleak House*
1857	*Little Dorrit*
1861	*Great Expectations*
1870	Death

This makes it easy to see that he was born as the U.S. entered the War of 1812 and died soon after the end of the Civil War. If you added other literary figures from the same period, you would not soon forget that Dickens, Dostoyesky, Tolstoy, Kierkegaard, Ibsen, Noah Webster, Emerson, Longfellow, Melville and Hawthorne, among many others, were all literary contemporaries. Adding nonliterary events to your timeline would enable you to make connections between what was being written and what was going on in the United States, Britain, Europe, Africa, etc.

Draw a concept tree

Another terrific device for limiting the amount of verbiage in your notes and making them more memorable is the concept tree. Like a time line, the concept tree is a visual representation of the relationship among several key facts. For instance, one might depict the categories and examples of musical instruments this way:

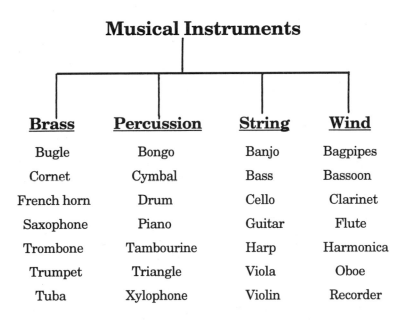

Musical Instruments

<u>Brass</u>	<u>Percussion</u>	<u>String</u>	<u>Wind</u>
Bugle	Bongo	Banjo	Bagpipes
Cornet	Cymbal	Bass	Bassoon
French horn	Drum	Cello	Clarinet
Saxophone	Piano	Guitar	Flute
Trombone	Tambourine	Harp	Harmonica
Trumpet	Triangle	Viola	Oboe
Tuba	Xylophone	Violin	Recorder

Such devices certainly give further credence to the old saying, "A picture is worth a thousand words," since time lines and concept trees will be much more helpful than mere words in remembering material, particularly conceptual material. Developing them will ensure that your interest in the text will not flag too much.

But don't limit yourself to just these two types of "pictures." Consider using a chart, graph, diagram or anything else you can think of to reorganize *any* information for *any* class you're taking (especially science, history or English).

The more extensive and difficult the information you need to understand, the more complex your "pictorial" summary may have to be. Rearranging information in this way will not only show connections you may have missed but also help you understand them better. It sure makes review easier!

Add a vocabulary list

Many questions on exams require students to define the terminology in a discipline. Your physics professor will want to know what vectors are, while your calculus teacher will want to know about differential equations. Your history professor will want you to be well-versed on the Cold War, and your English literature professor will require you to know about the Romantic Poets.

Therefore, as I read my textbooks, I was sure to write down all new terms and definitions in my notes and draw little boxes around them, because I knew these were among the most likely items to be asked about on tests, and that the box would always draw my attention to them when I was reviewing.

Most textbooks will provide definitions of key terms. If your textbook does *not* define a key term, however, make sure that you write the term down in your notes *with* its definition. Remember that your notes should reflect *your* individual understanding of the term. Take the time to rephrase and write it in your own words. This will help you remember it.

Wait, you're not done yet!

After you've finished making notes on a chapter, go through them and identify the most important points—the ones that might turn up on tests—either with an asterisk or by highlighting them. You'll probably end up marking about 40 or 50 percent of your entries.

When you're reviewing for a test, you should read all the notes, but your asterisks will indicate which points you considered the most important *while the chapter was fresh in your mind.*

To summarize, when it comes to taking notes from your texts or other reading material, you should:

- Take a cursory look through the chapter *before* you begin reading. Look for subheads, highlighted terms and summaries at the end of the chapter to give you a sense of the content.

- Read each section thoroughly. While your review of the chapter "clues" will help you to understand the material, you should read for comprehension rather than speed.

- Make notes immediately after you've finished reading, using the outline, time line and concept tree and vocabulary list methods of organizations as necessary.

- Mark with an asterisk or highlight the key points as you review your notes.

Chapter 7

Rembring how too spel gud

Every time I have my daughter read to me, I become aware of the difficulties of spelling in English. What's that "k" doing on the edge of the knife, and why didn't someone put the lights out on that "gh" in night? How come graffiti has two "f"s and one "t" while spaghetti doubles the "t" (and pronounces the "gh" as a hard "g"!)?

Well, one way to win the spelling bee in your town is to have a great vocabulary, using some of the suggestions mentioned in Chapter 5. Another way is to learn the rules of English spelling, then make special note of the rather frequent exceptions to those rules.

Double or nothing

Many people make mistakes on words with doubled consonants. The most common quick-repeating consonants are "l," "n," "p" and "s", but "t" and "r" repeat fairly often, too. While the incidence of these doubles might seem accidental or arbitrary, they usually follow these rules:

Double "l": Usually results from adding suffixes ending in "l" to roots beginning with the letter, vice versa for suffixes (examples: *alliterative, unusually*). However, alien does *not* have a double "l" because it is itself a root.
Double "n": A similar rule applies to "n"s. Double "n"s usually result from adding a suffix that turns an adjective ending in "n" into a noun (*wantonness* or *thinness*) or "-ny," which turns a noun ending in "n" into an adjective (*funny*).

Double "p,"s "r"s and "s"s don't generally have a hard-and-fast rule, so you'll usually have to rely on other tricks of memory. For instance, I've always had trouble spelling *embarrassment* (double "r" *and* double "s") since it certainly doesn't seem to follow the same rule as *harassment* (double "s" only).

In these cases, you'll have to associate some rule with the word. When I worked as a reporter, you'd often hear people answer questions about spelling in such codes. "Four 's's and two 'p's" is the answer to "How do you spell Mississippi?" I remember the rule for the word *harassment* by imagining someone pushing away (or harassing) the "r" some part of my brain insists should be there.

Double "r"s and double "t"s and other doubles occurring (note the double "r"!) before "-ed":

1. If the word ends in a single consonant (occuR, omiT)
2. If the word is accented on the last syllable (comPEL, reMIT)

Is it "i" before "e" or...?

The general rule is: "I" before "e" except after "c" or when it sounds like "a," as in "neighbor" and "weigh." This rule holds, with some exceptions: *seize, leisure, caffeine* and the names of other chemical compounds.

Honest "-able"

Many people get thrown over words ending in "e" that have "-able" or "-ible" added to them. What to do with that final "e"? Well, here are some rules:

- ***Keep the final "e"*** for words ending in "-ice," "-ace" or "-ge." Someone is embracEABLE and situations are managEABLE.
- ***Drop that final "e"*** when it is preceded by any consonant other than "c" or "g" (*unlovable*).

Other rules for adding suffixes to words ending in "e":

- Retain the "e" when adding "-ly" and "-ment" (unless the word ends in "-dge." It's *judgment, not* judgEment).
- Drop the "e" before adding "y" as a suffix (*phony*).
- Drop the final "e" and add "-ible" to words ending in "-nce," "-uce" or "-rce" (*producible, unconvincible*).
- Use "-ible" for words ending in "-miss" (*dismissible*).

Rules are meant to be broken

The English language is based on Celtic, Norwegian, German, Latin, French and several other languages. As a result, it veers from the rules fairly often. So, while these guidelines certainly will help you a great deal, sometimes you will have to rely on association and some of the other methods we spoke of in other chapters to remember all the *exceptions* to them.

Chapter 8

Remembering numbers the mnemonic way

Up until now, we've been dealing in the rich world of words. Anything having to do with words is a relatively easy task for the memory because words always can be associated with *things*, which, because they can be seen, touched, heard and smelled, can carry more than one association and, therefore, be easier to remember.

But a number is an abstraction. Unless associated with something, it is relatively difficult to remember. For instance, most people have tremendous difficulty remembering telephone numbers that they've only heard once. The reason is that a phone number doesn't usually conjure up an image or a sensation. It is merely seven or 10 digits without a relationship to one another or to you.

The trick, then, is to establish more associations for numbers.

But how? After all, they can be so abstract. It would be like trying to remember colors without having the benefit of *things* associated with those colors.

Making friends with numbers

Numbers are infinite, but the system we use to designate them is even more user-friendly than the alphabet. It consists of 10 digits that all of you should know by now (just follow the bouncing ball): 0, 1, 2, 3, 4, 5, 6, 7, 8 and 9.

The trick to the mnemonic alphabet—a rather popular technique for remembering numbers—is turning those numbers into the equivalent of letters, symbols that represent sounds. The pioneer of this concept is Harry Lorayne, author of many books on memory. His method calls for associating the 10 familiar Arabic numerals with a sound or a related group of sounds.

Here's how this brilliantly simple scheme works:

1 = T, D
2 = N
3 = M
4 = R
5 = L
6 = J, soft G, CH, SH, DG, TCH
7 = K, hard C, hard G, Q
8 = F, V, PH
9 = P, B
0 = Z, soft C, S

You're probably thinking, "What sense does this all make, and how in heck am I supposed to remember it?"

Well, though this seems like madness, believe me, there's some extraordinarily wonderful method in it.

The number one is a single downstroke, as is the letter "T." "D" is a suitable substitute because it is pronounced almost the same way as "T"—by touching the tongue to the front of the roof of the mouth.

"N" represents two because "N" has two downstrokes.

"M" is a stand-in for three because, you guessed it, it has three downstrokes.

Four is represented by "R" because the dominant sound in the word *four* is the "-RRRRRR" at the end.

The Romans used "L" to represent 50. Also, if you fan out the fingers of your left hand as if to say, "It's 5 o'clock," your index finger and thumb form the letter "L."

Hold a mirror up to a six and you get a "J," particularly if you write as badly as I do. Therefore, all letters pronounced like "J"—by touching your tongue to the inside of your lower teeth—are acceptable substitutes for six.

Place two sevens back to back, turning one upside down, and what do you have? Right, a "K." All of those letter sounds formed in the back of the mouth, as is "K," are therefore potential substitutes for the lucky seven.

Draw a line parallel to the ground through a handwritten eight and you will create a symbol that resembles a script, lower case "F." Therefore, all sounds formed by placing the top teeth on the lower lip can represent eight.

Once again, I invoke my mirror, mirror on the wall to show that a nine and a capital "P" are virtually identical. "B," also formed by putting your lips together, is a substitute for nine anytime.

Zero is an easy one. Zero begins with a "Z," so any sound formed by hissing through the space between flat tongue and roof of mouth is acceptable.

Now what?

Believe me, this device, which probably seems very ungainly to you now, is a terrific way to remember numbers. Go over the list above a few more times, cover it up, and take the little quiz below, matching numbers with appropriate sounds and vice-versa:

6 _____

B _____

F _____

2 _____

L _____

Q _____

9 _____

S _____

J _____

7 _____

Consonantal divide

Have you noticed that all of the sounds used in the mnemonic alphabet are consonants? That's because users of the system should be free to use vowels however they please around these consonants to form words or memorable sounds. Therefore the number 15 can be "QueeN." Or the number of that wonderful person you met in the Rathskeller today and would so like to see again could be "vasectomy to go," or 806-1316 (VSCTMTG).

How about trying to remember pi to seven places. You could try to memorize 3.141592 or just think, "MeTRic TalL PeNny."

Is it easier to remember your social security number (say, 152-40-1821) or "TelL NoRa SaDie PHoNeD"?

A great date

One of the most useful applications of this method is remembering dates and tying them to events. If you wanted to remember, for example, "William the Conqueror invaded England in 1066," you could endlessly repeat that sentence, or you could remember, "Bill THiS eGG." Combining these methods with the chain-link technique we discussed in earlier chapters, you could imagine an egg rolling off the white cliffs of Dover, where William first landed. (Alternately, you can make up a ridiculous but simple rhyme like, "In 1066, Billy C ate fish and chips" that would also work just fine.)

Now you try it. Make up phrases using the mnemonic alphabet equivalents for your Social Security number, the first three phone numbers in your little black book or the times for high and low tide tomorrow. Then try the quiz, writing in first the letter equivalents for the numbers, then a brief word, phrase or sentence that would help you remember it. I've done the first one for you.

844941   FRRPRT   FuRRy PoRT
                        (or FuRRy PRiDe)

671024

95770002

84712457

746603201

1234567890

0967854213

What about even longer numbers? How do you remember 20-, 30-, even 50-digit numbers without trying too
hard? Well, you could make your "story sentences" longer.
But you can also group the numbers into a series of pictures. For example, let's say you had to remember the
number 289477500938199101550—that's 21 digits! Try
grouping it into smaller number combinations, creating a
picture for each. In this case, I've managed with only two
pictures:

289477 can be represented by NVPRGK or a
picture of a sailor (NaVy) PouRing GunK.

500938 is LZZBMV. How is the sailor standing?
LaZily. Where is he standing? Right By a MoVie
theatre. (See it in your head.)

199101550. What is playing at the theatre?
DeBBie DoeS DaLLaS. (Now you know why he
wasn't paying attention to the gunk!)

Can you see how you could easily memorize a 50-digit
number with just four or five pictures? Try it yourself.
You'll see how easy it is.

Everybody loves them dead presidents

Or so sang bluesman Willie Dixon, referring to the
presidential portraits that grace our folding money. But he
could just as easily have been referring to your least favorite history professor—you know, the one who expects you
to know who was the 23rd president of the United States?
By the way, that was Harrison, and the way we will remember that is "No ('N' represents 2), My ('M' is for 3)
hairy son."

Now you try it. Here are the dozen most recent U.S.
vice presidents. How are you going to remember them?

34. Harry Truman
35. Alben Barkley
36. Richard Nixon
37. Lyndon Johnson
38. Hubert Humphrey
39. Spiro Agnew
40. Gerald Ford
41. Nelson Rockefeller
42. Walter Mondale
43. George Bush
44. Dan Quayle
45. Al Gore

How did you do?

Here's how I would use mnemonics to establish a chain link between names and numbers:

Truman:	"Meet MR (34) true, man."
Quayle:	Picture a RoaRing (44) quail.
Mondale:	Picture a Jamaican Ayrdale (mon) RuNning (42)
Ford:	Picture a brand-new Ford RiSing (40) in the air.

Get the idea? This is an absolutely invaluable tool. It will empower you to remember phone numbers without resorting to writing on wet cocktail napkins. Perhaps more important, it will help you remember dates and facts without incessantly repeating them.

Chapter 9

Remembering names and faces

Like it or not, you're not going to be in school for the rest of your life. Soon, you will begin to look for a job, to string together a network of acquaintances and contacts that will help lift you onto that first rung of the corporate ladder.

You'll participate in that horrible convention called the cocktail party and other social events where you'll be expected to be charming.

Every once in a while, I go to a cocktail party, if only to remind myself why I don't do it more often. But seriously, cocktail parties give me a chance to practice a skill that I consider one of the key reasons for my earlier success as an advertising salesperson: remembering the names (and some of the other pertinent personal data) that went with the faces.

In fact, one of the principal reasons I became interested in the subject of memory improvement was that I was tired of calling people "pal" and "buddy" when I could *not* remember their names after they said to *me,* "Hey, Ron, how have you been?"

You can avoid those embarrassing moments forever by memorizing these key steps to link a person's face and name in your memory forever.

Take a good look

Whenever you meet someone, look him or her in the face and make special note of some outstanding feature. Does the person have a big nose? Huge earlobes? Dimples? Big, beautiful blue eyes? A cleft in the chin? A mole? It doesn't have to be a particularly ugly or beautiful feature— just something that sets the person apart from the rest of the people in the room.

Once you've locked in on a feature, do *not* stare at it, but *do* get your imagination working—make that feature truly outstanding by embellishing it. If it's a big nose, make it as big as a toucan's beak in your mind's eye. Dimples should be as large as craters; big earlobes should dangle on the person's shoulders.

Make sure you got it

I remember once introducing my friend Tony to three people who, along with him, were the first to arrive at my house for a little dinner party. One minute later, I went into the kitchen to fix drinks for everybody and Tony was right at my heels. "What was the name of that brunette in the miniskirt?" he asked in a hushed voice. "Monique," I said. "How 'bout the bald guy?" asked Tony. "That's Joe." Finally, very embarrassed, Tony asked, "And what about the other woman?"

There are fleas with longer memories. But now Tony prides himself on being able to remember the names of 30 or 40 people in a room after being introduced only once.

The first thing he taught himself to do was to repeat the person's name, looking right at him or her as he did so. Tony, being a very charming guy, doesn't do this as if he's trying out for a lead role in the remake of *Being There*. He repeats the name back as part of a greeting—"Nice to meet you, Monique." "Hi Joe, I've heard a lot about you. You're Ron's partner, right?"

Using such a technique, you will not only be noting the person's name, you will be making sure that you got it right.

Think of a link

Once you've done that, it's time to come up with some sort of link between the name and the feature that you've already exaggerated out of proportion.

I saw the most obvious example of this as a kid when a memorist appeared on a Sunday morning TV show. He was introduced to the 100 or so youngsters in the audience and repeated all of their names back to them at the end of the show. Asked how he had done it, he used the example of a boy named Tommy Fox. The boy had a dimple, said the memorist, so he imagined a bare meadow with a hole in the middle. A fox bounded through the hedge followed by hunters shouting, "Tommy Ho!"

Bingo! The name and the face were linked forever.

Too easy, you say?

There are much *easier* ones. Before you go too far afield creating a memorable mental picture, don't overlook the obvious. Some names are so memorable you shouldn't have to work too hard—try "Boomer" Esiason (okay, you *might* have to work on "Esiason") or Chip Dale (gotta love those chipmunks). Other first or last names should *automatically* trigger specific pictures—a flower (Rose, Daisy, Hyacinth), a piece of jewelry (Amber, Ruby, Jasper, Opal,

Pearl, Jade, Ivory), an object (Gates, Ford, Bentley, Royce, Zipper, Glass, Cross, Brook, River, Pen, Pack, Beam, Tent, *ad infinitum*), a profession (Tinker, Taylor, Soldier, Spy), a city or town (Clifton, Springfield, Austin, Houston, Dallas, Savannah, York), a familiar street, the name of your favorite team, a breed of dog or cat.

Some names differing by only a letter could use such objects as links—Pack to remember Gregory *Peck*, Pen for Sean *Penn*, Tent for *Trent*, Road for Rhodes or, for a little more stretch, Tombs for *Thomas*, Cow for *Cowher* (Go, Steelers!).

Your associations could take advantage of your own particular knowledge. Small for *Klein*, if you know German; tie-ins to your favorite sports figure or movie star or author; an association with terms endemic to your profession. The list of possible tie-ins is absolutely endless.

If you *still* can't think of such a link, you can always rhyme: Wallets for *Wallace*, Georgie Porgie, Bad Chad, Freaky Frank, Ron Ron weighs a ton.

Once you've come up with these soundalikes or pictures, find some way to link them with the image you've formed of the person's chief facial features.

For instance, once I was introduced to a man named Vince Dolce (pronounced Dole-see). As I was walking toward him, I noticed some rather dark circles under his eyes. In my imagination, because I'm so accustomed to using the technique outlined above, the circles became bigger than a raccoon's. When I heard that his name was Dolce, I immediately thought, "dull sheep" and pictured tired, sleepy sheep grazing on those now even bigger circles below Vince's eyes. The sheep, of course, were bothering him, and this made him *wince* (for Vince).

That's all there is to turning a room full of strangers into people that—for better or worse—you'll never forget!

Chapter 10

Remembering a speech or oral report

The English poet John Donne wrote, "Death be not proud," and no wonder: In many public opinion polls in which respondents were asked to rate their biggest fears, public speaking—not the grim reaper—won...hands down.

The reasons for this are many, but undoubtedly heading the list is the horrible idea that in mid-sentence we will go blank, completely unable to recall the brilliant speech we'd stayed up writing late the night before.

We'll return to our seat in a muddled silence. Feeling like a naked person in a spotlight.

To make sure that doesn't happen to you, I'll teach you how to use chain links, association and all of the other tricks we've discussed in this book to help you remember speeches or oral class presentations.

Take note

Remember the outline method we spoke about in Chapter 6? Well, the way to go about preparing a speech is to outline it, write it, *re*outline it and then use the outline as your key to remembering it. Why should you bother when you went through the trouble of writing the speech in the first place?

Well, because there are two kinds of speakers: good and dull. The good ones *talk* to you. The bad ones *read* to you. In order to be a *speaker*, rather than a *reader*, you should know your speech by heart.

A tasty toastmaster

Let's step aside from the memory issue and talk about how you should organize your speech (after all, it will be the key to remembering it well).

I've done so much public speaking throughout my career that I've actually grown to enjoy it—in fact, I look *forward* to talking to a room full of strangers. I don't think that would be the case at all were it not for a piece of valuable advice I acquired quite a few years ago. There is only one best way to organize a speech: Tell them what you are going to say; say it; then, tell them what you said.

Let's say you were assigned to take one side of an argument in a debate and your topic is, "The solution to the drug problem: Legalize all drugs." Your outline might look something like this:

The opening
I.   Drugs should be legalized
II. This will help solve, not deepen, the drug crisis in the country
III. Keeping drugs illegal assures that criminals get rich and government funds go to waste

The middle

I. The reasons to legalize drugs
   A. Keeping them illegal artificially raises prices—costs are inflated 2,500 percent
   B. Public funds are being wasted
      1. Law enforcement efforts are not working
      2. Funds for rehabilitation are paltry
II. Control would be easier
   A. It has worked in other countries
   B. Licensing would increase state revenues
   C. Harsh penalties would inhibit sales to minors
   D. Drug addicts available for outreach programs
III. Prohibition doesn't work—parallels with Roaring Twenties

The closing

I. The costly, ineffective War on Drugs
II. Legalization sounds radical, but it would work
III. The alternative is far more dangerous

Commit it to memory

Once you have the outline, use the chain link method to remember the flow of your speech.

Here's how it might work for the outline above: First, you'd remember your opening by picturing yourself at an opening—a doorway, or maybe opening night of a play entitled, *Drug Free America*. Imagine yourself walking inside the theater and seeing three scenes set from left to right:

I. Congress enacting a law
II. People emerging from hospital beds and saying they don't need drugs anymore
III. Criminal types having piles of money taken from them by police

Next, you imagine yourself sitting in the *middle* section of the theater.

I. You look at your *Playbill* and it reads
    A. "2,500%"
    B. On the stage you see
        1. Police in handcuffs
        2. A nurse in a clinic begging for money
        3. A schoolroom with no teacher
II. Imagine some sort of control to remember this part of your exposition section, perhaps your foot on a gas pedal
    A. Your foot is on the gas pedal because you're driving past an Amsterdam street or a windmill (since Holland has a model program of legalization and control)
    B. You reach for your driver's license, which has a big dollar sign on it
    C. Out the window you see a seedy character being dragged from a schoolyard by the police
    D. You see that nurse in the clinic helping someone

Then, all of a sudden, you car is cut off by gangsters being chased by police as if in a classic car chase from *The Untouchables*. Then, imagine yourself closing your car door and hearing:

I.   The sounds of war. You look up and you see huge dollar signs suspended on parachutes coming down from the sky.
II. You see Karl Marx (or another "radical") in an army outfit and then,
III. A mushroom cloud or some other apocalyptic image.

Once you've conjured up a set of hooks like this, read your speech several times, mentally flipping through the appropriate images as you do so. In that way your words and ideas will become *linked* to pictures, making them so much easier to remember.

Get the picture?

The whole key to a good memory is establishing tags, links, associations—anything that will help your mind reel the memories in from the deep abyss of your memory banks.

The point of this chapter and all the others in this book is to show you how simple this can be. The rest is up to you. Developing a good memory requires you to practice the techniques I've discussed throughout this book.

After you've done so, you'll be more likely to get higher grades on exams that test your knowledge of facts. What's more, you might never forget where your keys, wallet or glasses are again.

I'd advise you to go back and read through Chapters 3 through 9 again, make conscious use of the techniques and then take the test in Chapter 12. If you do your homework, you'll probably score high.

Good luck!

Chapter 11

Let's not forget ADD

We both fear and pity kids on illegal drugs. But we also must face and deal with what's happening to the three million-plus who are on a legal drug—Ritalin, the prescribed drug of choice for kids diagnosed with Attention Deficit Disorder (ADD), hyperactivity or the combination of the two (ADHD). I could write a book on ADD, which seems to be the "diagnosis of choice" for school kids these days.

Luckily, I don't have to. Thom Hartmann has already written an excellent one—*Attention Deficit Disorder: A Different Perception*—from which I have freely and liberally borrowed (with his permission) for this chapter.

I'm going to have to leave others to debate whether ADD actually exists as a clearly definable illness, whether it's the "catchall" diagnosis of lazy doctors, whether teachers are labeling kids as ADD to avoid taking responsibility for students' poor learning skills, whether Ritalin is a miracle drug or one that is medicating creative kids into a conforming stupor.

All of these positions *have* been asserted and, as hundreds of new kids are medicated every day, the debate about ADD is only likely to continue...and heat up. That is not my concern in this book.

What I want to deal with here is the reality that many kids, however they're labeled, have severe problems in dealing with school as it usually exists. I want to give them the advice they need to contend with the symptoms that have acquired the label "ADD."

Some definitions, please

Just what is ADD? It's probably easiest to describe as a person's difficulty focusing on a simple thing for any significant amount of time. People with ADD are described as easily distracted, impatient, impulsive and often seeking immediate gratification. They have poor listening skills and have trouble doing "boring" jobs (like sitting quietly in class or, as adults, balancing a checkbook). "Disorganized" and "messy" are words that also come up often.

Hyperactivity is more clearly defined as restlessness, resulting in excessive activity. Hyperactives are usually described as having "ants in their pants." ADHD, the first category recognized in medicine some 75 years ago, is a combination of hyperactivity and ADD.

According to the American Psychiatric Association, a person has ADHD if he or she meets eight or more of the following paraphrased criteria:

1. Can't remain seated if required to do so.
2. Easily distracted by extraneous stimuli.
3. Focusing on a single task or play activity is difficult.
4. Frequently begins another activity without completing the first.

5. Fidgets or squirms (or feels restless mentally).
6. Can't (or doesn't want to) wait for his turn during group activities.
7. Will often interrupt with an answer before a question is completed.
8. Has problems with chore or job follow-through.
9. Can't play quietly easily.
10. Impulsively jumps into physically dangerous activities without weighing the consequences.
11. Easily loses things (pencils, tools, papers) necessary to complete school or work projects.
12. Interrupts others inappropriately.
13. Talks impulsively or excessively.
14. Doesn't seem to listen when spoken to.

Three caveats to keep in mind: The behaviors must have started before age 7, not represent some other form of classifiable mental illness and occur more frequently than in the average person of the same age.

Characteristics of people with ADD

Let's look at the characteristics generally ascribed to people with ADD in more detail:

Easily distracted. Since ADD people are constantly "scoping out" everything around them, focusing on a single item is difficult. Just try having a conversation with an ADD person while a television is on.

Short, but very intense, attention span. Though it can't be defined in terms of minutes or hours, anything ADD people find boring immediately loses their attention. Other projects may hold their rapt and extraordinarily intense attention for hours or days.

Disorganization. ADD children are often chronically disorganized—their rooms are messy, their desks are a shambles, their files incoherent. While people without ADD can be equally messy and disorganized, they can usually find what they are looking for; ADDers *can't*.

Distortions of time-sense. ADDers have an exaggerated sense of urgency when they're working on something and an exaggerated sense of boredom when they have nothing interesting to do.

Difficulty following directions. A new theory on this aspect holds that ADDers have difficulty processing auditory or verbal information. A major aspect of this difficulty involves the very-common reports of parents of ADD kids who say their kids love to watch TV and hate to read.

Daydreaming, falling into depressions or having mood swings.

Take risks. ADDers seem to make faster decisions than non-ADDers. This is why Thom Hartmann and Wilson Harrell, former publisher of *Inc.* magazine and author of *For Entrepreneurs Only*, conclude the vast majority of successful entrepreneurs probably have ADD! They call them "Hunters," as opposed to the more staid "Farmer" types.

Easily frustrated and impatient. ADDers do not suffer fools gladly. They are direct and to-the-point. When things aren't working, "Do something!" is the ADD rallying cry, even if that something is a bad idea.

Why ADD kids have trouble in school

First and foremost, says Thom Hartmann, schools are set up for "Farmers"—sit at a desk, do what you're told, watch and listen to the teacher. This is pure hell for the "Hunters" with ADD. The bigger the class size, the worse it becomes. Kids with ADD, remember, are easily distracted, bored, turned off, always ready to move on.

What should you look for in a school setting to make it more palatable to an ADD son or daughter? What can you do at home to help your child (or yourself)? Hartmann has some solid answers.

- **Learning needs to be project- and experience-based**, providing more opportunities for creativity and shorter and smaller "bites" of information. many "gifted" programs offer exactly such opportunities. The problem for many kids with ADD is that they've spent years in nongifted, farmer-type classroom settings and may be labeled with underachieving behavior problems, effectively shut out of the programs virtually designed for them! Many parents report that children diagnosed as ADD, who failed miserably in public school, thrived in private school. Hartmann attributes this to the smaller classrooms, more individual attention with specific goal-setting, project-based learning and similar methods common in such schools. These factors are just what make ADD kids thrive!

- **Create a weekly performance template** on which *both* teacher and parent chart the child's performance, positive and negative. "Creating such a larger-than-the-child system," claims Hartmann, "will help keep ADD children on task and on time."

- **Encourage special projects for extra credit.** Projects give ADDers the chance to learn in the mode that's most appropriate for them. They will also give such kids the chance to make up for the "boring" homework they sometimes simply can't make themselves do.

- **Stop labeling them "disordered."** Kids react to labels, especially negative ones, even more than adults. Saying "you have a deficit and a disorder" may be more destructive than useful.

- **Think twice about medication**, but don't discard the option. Hartmann has a concern about the long-term side effects of drugs normally prescribed for ADDers. He notes that they may well be more at risk to be substance abusers as adults, so starting them on medication at a young age sends a very mixed message. However, if an ADD child cannot have his or her special needs met in a classroom, *not* medicating him or her may be a disaster. "The relatively unknown long-term risks of drug therapy," says Hartmann, "may be more than offset by the short-term benefits of improved classroom performance."

Specific suggestions for remembering

- **Practice, practice, practice** the memory techniques in this book. ADDers tend to have trouble listening and are easily distracted. As a result, they may fail to remember things they simply never heard or paid attention to. Work on the visualization techniques. Practice making mental pictures when having conversations; create mental images of your "to-do" list; visualize doing things to which you've committed or for which you are receiving instructions or directions. Practice careful listening skills. Many of Harry Lorayne's memory books (especially his classic, *The Memory Book*), which stress "picture-oriented" approaches to memory problems, would be invaluable additions to any ADDer's library.

- **Write everything down.** This is something I recommend everyone doing, but it is absolutely essential for ADDers. The more you write down, the less you have to remember!

- **Utilize pictures, mapping, diagrams**, etc., in lieu of outlines or "word" notes—even the abbreviations and shorthand I've recommended in *Take Notes*.

- **Tape record lectures**, despite what I wrote in *How to Study*. This will enable them to relisten and reprocess information they may have missed the first time around.

- **Create distraction-free zones.** Henry David Thoreau (who evidently suffered from ADD, by the way) was so desperate to escape distraction he moved to isolated Walden Pond. Organize your time and workspace to create your own "Walden Pond," especially when you have to write, take notes, read or study. ADDers need silence, so consider the library. Another tip: Clean your work area thoroughly at the end of each day. This will minimize distractions.

- **Train your attention span.** ADDers will probably never be able to train themselves to ignore distractions totally, but a variety of meditation techniques might help them stay focused longer.

Chapter 12

Test your progress

As promised, I'm going to give you a chance to check your progress. If you've studied the contents of this book thoroughly and have made an effort to put some of its advice to work, you should score much higher now than you did on the quiz in Chapter 2.

Test #1: the mnemonic alphabet

Study this number for 30 seconds. Then cover it up and replicate as much as you can, taking only another 20 seconds or so.

628891247324518270964

Test #2: a better vocabulary

Here are a number of obscure vocabulary words and their meanings. Study them for no more than three minutes, then answer the questions below.

1. **Roux:** A cooked mixture of butter or other fat and flour used to thicken soups, sauces, etc.

2. **Bregma:** The place on the top of the skull where the frontal bone and parietal bones join.

3. **Crimple:** To wrinkle or curl; crinkle.

4. **Litmus:** A blue coloring matter obtained from certain lichens.

5. **Longicorn:** Having long antennae.

6. **Naos:** A temple or shrine.

7. **Resplendent:** Shining brilliantly; gleaming.

8. **Serry:** To crowd closely together.

9. **Withershins:** Counterclockwise.

10. **Decuple:** Ten times as great.

11. **Brock:** European badger.

12. **Adscititious:** Derived from an external source; additional.

13. **Epizoic:** Living on the surface of an animal.

14. **Tantara:** A blast of a trumpet or horn.

15. **Ophiology:** The study of snakes.

16. **Cognoscenti:** Well informed persons, especially those who have superior knowledge of a particular field, particularly the arts.

17. **Divagate:** To wander; stray.

18. **Marplot:** A person who spoils a plot, design or project by meddling.

19. **Vespine:** Pertaining to wasps.

20. **Mome:** A fool; blockhead.

Okay, cover them up and take this test:

1. Something 10 times as great is called _____.

2. Did you see that cute _____ poking his face out of the ground?

3. _____ is another word for counterclockwise.

4. The meeting had a tendency to _____ from the agenda.

5. Something is "epizoic" if it can live on _____.

6. The extra money must have come from an _____ source.

7. Let's all _____ together under the awning until it stops raining.

8. A mome is a A) fool or a B) genius?

9. Everybody went to the _____ on the night before the holy festival.

10. The look in her eyes was as _____ as the diamond he presented to her.

11. _____ is a blue coloring matter from certain lichens.

12. New Orleans cooks use a lot of _____ in their recipes.

13. A creature with long antennae is _____.

14. Be very careful when handling the baby; the _____ is a very sensitive spot on the head.

15. Studying the _____ world is fascinating; I never realized how different wasps are from bees.

16. It seemed like the panel of _____ enjoyed his performance, although he was only an amateur.

17. The new fabric is delicate and may _____.

18. My boyfriend is studying _____, but I have to admit, I'm afraid of reptiles.

19. A blast from the _____ awakened everyone in the village.

20. Someone who meddles, spoiling plans, can be called a _____.

Test #3: dates & events

Study the following dates, events and facts. Then take the test on the next page.

1967: London Bridge is moved to Arizona.

1876: Alexander Graham Bell invents the telephone.

Harvard, oldest university in the U.S., was founded in 1636.

With an annual rainfall of 3.73 inches, Nevada is the driest state in the Union.

President McKinley was assassinated in 1901.

Congress passed the Tonkin Gulf Resolution, increasing American involvement in the Vietnam War, in 1964.

George Washington was inaugurated in Philadelphia in 1789.

The horrific battle of Gettysburg was fought in 1863.

30,000 people work in the Pentagon building.

Eli Whitney invented the cotton gin in 1793.

Jamestown, the first permanent European settlement in the New World, was founded in 1607.

The Korean War, though never officially declared, raged from 1950 to 1953.

continued...

Pilgrims signed the Mayflower Compact in 1620.

Thomas Jefferson purchased the Louisiana Territory from Napoleon in 1803.

Now answer the following questions:

1. The cotton gin was invented when and by whom?

2. The Battle of Gettysburg raged in what year?

3. How many people live in California?

4. In what year was Jamestown founded?

5. How many inches of rain fall on the driest state of the Union? What state is it?

6. What is the name and founding date of the oldest university in the United States?

7. George Washington was inaugurated in Philadelphia. In what year did it occur?

8. When and by whom was the telephone invented?

9. When and to what state was the London Bridge moved?

10. How many people work in the Pentagon?

11. When did America enter into full-scale conflict in Vietnam?

12. When did Teddy Roosevelt succeed McKinley?

13. America became the proud owner of New Orleans in what year?

14. When did the Korean War take place?

15. When did the Pilgrims sign the Mayflower Compact?

Test #4: reading retention

Scan the following paragraphs excerpted from *Taking the Mystery Out of TQM* (Career Press, 1995), in order to answer the questions that follow (which you may read first). The answers are at the end of Test 4. This should take you no more than two minutes:

The Taguchi Loss Function demonstrates a formula to determine the cost of a lack of quality. According to the Loss Function, for each deviation there is an incremental economic loss of some geometric proportion. The cumulative impact can be great for a number of parts deviating just a little. This differs from the traditional view which states that there is no real detrimental impact as long as parts are produced within engineering tolerances or specifications.

Think of this concept in the management of a company. Consider the interrelationships and interdependence among finance, marketing, sales and information systems. Each group has developed procedures to achieve its goals. In order for each to perform optimally, all work from other departments must be understood and integrated into a flow chart to reflect the integrity of the whole.

According to Taguchi, if all systems and schedules are off only slightly, there is probably little impact on any one individual or even one department. Taken collectively, however, the toll will be far greater. Even if each department missed each of its deadlines by only a single day, the impact could well be a product that is too late for the customer who ordered it.

1. If each department misses its deadline by one day, the result could be:

    A. Increased productivity.

    B. Grand scale layoffs.

    C. The product is too late.

    D. Unnoticeable.

2. The Taguchi Loss Function demonstrates a formula to determine:

    A. Employee attitudes.

    B. The effects of poor quality.

    C. Praise or insults.

    D. Office partnerships.

3. The author compares the Taguchi Loss Function to:

    A. Group dynamics.

    B. Geometry.

    C. Scheduling.

    D. Company management.

4. The traditional view states that:

    A. The cumulative impact can be great for a number of parts deviating just a little.

    B. Each group has developed procedures to achieve its goals.

    C. There is no detrimental impact so long as parts are produced with engineering tolerances or specifications.

    D. For each deviation, there is an incremental loss of some geometric proportion.

Now read the following passage and answer the questions that follow (but do not look at the questions first). Give yourself four minutes for this exercise:

Five major scandals tainted the administration of President Ulysses S. Grant. Although the hero of Vicksburg was the first President to encounter charges of substantial wrongdoing during his administration, it was never proved that he was directly involved in any criminal acts nor that he profited from any of the acts of others.

The first incident occurred in 1869, the first year of his presidency. Known as Black Friday, it involved speculators James Fisk and Jay Gould and their attempt to corner the gold market. By involving Grant's brother-in-law, they hoped to prevent the government from "dumping" its gold onto the market, which would make it impossible for their scheme to succeed. Grant was not directly involved in Fisk's and Gould's machinations, but he gave the appearance of complicity, allowing himself to be entertained lavishly and publicly on Fisk's yacht. However, when the pair's aggressive gold purchases sent its price skyrocketing in a matter of days, Grant acted swiftly, ordering the Treasury Department to sell off $4 million in gold reserves. While this ended Fisk's and Gould's attempt, this step brought ruin to a number of individuals and businesses that were "riding the wave" of gold fever and resulted in a national economic shock not matched until the 1929 stock market crash.

The second major scandal involved the embezzlement of massive amounts of money by the Credit Mobilier holding company, which was involved with the construction of the Union Pacific railway. To avoid being discovered, the conspirators heavily bribed members of Congress and officials of the Republican Party, of which Grant was the nominal head. Although this scandal erupted during a heated reelection campaign against newspaper publisher Horace Greeley, Grant was evidently completely uninvolved and was reelected handily.

Two other scandals involved taxes and officials appointed to collect them. One tax collector, John Sanborn, managed to keep nearly half of the delinquent taxes he collected, a total that exceeded $200,000. That paled in comparison to the fraud discovered by Treasury Secretary Benjamin H. Bristow among liquor distillers and the officials charged with collecting taxes from them. Although Grant called for swift action against the conspirators, his fervor flagged when his trusted personal secretary, Orville Babcock, was implicated in the scheme. Grant then slowed the investigation, but 110 conspirators were eventually found guilty.

In the final year of Grant's second term, evidence mounted that Secretary of War W.W. Belknap had been taking bribes from white traders at Indian trading posts. Since Grant had made much of his earlier attempts to institute a fair and nonabusive set of policies toward the Indians, the scandal was a personal embarrassment, though, again, Grant was in no way directly involved. Faced with certain impeachment, Belknap resigned.

1. In what year did the Credit Mobilier embezzlement become public?

2. In what year did Belknap resign?

3. Approximately how much tax revenue did John D. Sanborn collect before he was caught?

None of these answers are directly stated in the selection, though all can be easily inferred from it. The answers are: 1) 1872, if the first year of Grant's presidency was 1869, then the reelection campaign is 1872. The previous election occurred in 1868. Election years are always divisible by four; 2) 1876, the final year of Grant's second term; see above for reasoning; 3) $400,000. (He kept "nearly half of the taxes he collected, for a total that exceeded $200,000.)

Answers to the first part of Test 4:

    1. C   3. D
    2. B   4. C

Test #5: remembering lists, however obscure

Study the first two lists for one minute each, then close the book and recite them back. Do the same for the third and fourth lists, except allow three minutes for the third, five minutes for the fourth:

Dances: Farruca, carol, jota, redowa, hoolachan, malaguena, tarantella, valeta, bourree, allemande.

Alcoholic drinks: oloroso, fino, bingo, sack, geropiga, catawba, demerara, arak, usquebaugh, zythum, twankay.

Cheeses: Derby, Gloucester, stracchino, Red Windsor, Bel Paese, Esrom, Feta, Vacherin, Wexford, Caerphilly, sapsago, Gammelost, Crowdie, Chevrotin, Lymeswold, Pultost, Raclette, Blarney, Edam, Havarti, Mysost, Islay.

Ships or vessels: Monoxylon, drake, whiff, packet, lymphad, galley, carrack, bawley, praam, randan, sub, razee, geordie, felucca, bireme, coracle, dinghy, skiff, sloop, grab, coaster, brigantine, saic, tern, tub, tug, fore-and-after, masoolah, puteli, shallop, patamar, gallivat, dogger, gondola, butty, budgerow.

Test #6: the rules of English spelling

Identify the misspelled words in the following list:

Dissatisfied

Immediately

Stoney

Likeable

Receeve

Measurement

Liesure

Commited

Occurence

Compeling

Harrasment

Embarassment

Drunkeness

Unconvincible

Regretible

Mistake

Mistatement

How did you do? (See the bottom of this page for the spelling solutions.)

I hope that you scored well and are confident that you can approach your schoolwork—and the rest of your life, inside and outside of school—with the assurance that your memory will be an ally rather than a foil.

In the above list, the following are the only words spelled *correctly*: stoney (though stony is preferred), likeable, mistake, dissatisfied, unconvincible, immediately and measurement.

Index